BETTER *AND* FASTER

BETTER *AND* FASTER

The Proven Path to Unstoppable Ideas

JEREMY GUTSCHE

CURRENCY
NEW YORK

SHELAGH GUTSCHE:

This book is dedicated to you, my champion of a mother, for everything you've done to raise two happy, motivated, entrepreneurial kids while teaching us the importance of family, friends, and understanding people.

Contents

PROLOGUE

P *aper planes, rocket ships, human hearts, and origami.* These are seemingly unrelated elements, but not to Robert Lang, an origami expert-for-hire who uses the power of paper-folding to save lives. Many of us have folded a few paper planes in our day, but Lang turned the ancient Asian craft into his life's passion. His peculiar journey began in the first grade, when his teacher gave him an origami art book. She hoped the quirky challenge would keep him from distracting his peers. She was right. Lang became obsessed over his newfound folding hobby.

Origami may be fun, but many will see the pursuit as frivolous. What Lang's teachers didn't realize was that with each paper plane pleated and each origami crane crafted, Lang came closer to unlocking secrets that would transform him into a leading innovator in aerospace, heart surgery, and automotive engineering. What did Lang see that others didn't? He started seeing more than just the art.

He saw the patterns.

Patterns surround us. We eat them, see them, smell them, taste them, and walk past them every day. But most people fail to connect the dots. They don't recognize ideas that others will relate to, gaps in service, or niches where one can rake in profits simply by diverging from the mainstream.

For Lang, the patterns were inescapable, especially when he delved deeper into the art of paper folding, a traditional hobby that had been stagnant for centuries and seemingly limited in scope.

Certain shapes were considered too difficult to re-create, such as spiders, bugs, or beetles. But those limits only challenged Lang's imagination. He was enthralled by impossibilities. He didn't know it at the time, but this was his awakening.

By day, Lang studied electrical engineering at Stanford and eventually earned a PhD at Caltech, writing his thesis on "Semiconductor Lasers: New Geometries and Spectral Properties." His doctoral work was unrelated to his art, but away from his academic pursuits, he studied the Japanese origami greats and taught himself to fold excruciatingly difficult constructions, including a paper Jimmy Carter and Darth Vader. He wanted to fold fire ants, hermit crabs, and dragons, but these feats remained beyond his grasp.

Origami was an all-consuming hobby.

Post-PhD, Lang became a talented fiber-optic researcher, but during his off-hours, he fed his hunger for origami, joining the competitive underworld of Japanese origami. His accomplishments earned him acceptance into the Origami Detectives, a Japanese-based alliance of paper-folders who dared to dream of unthinkably intricate folding feats, such as creating a horned winged beetle.

Work and play soon merged. Laboring with the intensity of a mad scientist, Lang began to see the science behind his origami. He discovered that all shapes follow a few predictable patterns, a truth that had been overlooked for centuries. And he developed a software program to calculate the folding pattern of almost any figure imaginable: He would input a simple stick drawing into the program, and the software would spell out the folds needed to craft what was previously thought to be impossible. His fellow paper-folders called it "The Secret Weapon."

Lang revolutionized origami. Finally, he was able to fold the coveted winged spotted beetle. Suddenly, the degree of difficulty in origami competitions skyrocketed, with the average number of folds per paper tripling from thirty to a hundred.

Despite having secured forty-six patents in optoelectronics, at the age of forty, Lang abandoned his successful career in fiber-optic research to *fold* full time.[1] He dedicated his life to hunting unexplored origami opportunities. "There were plenty of people doing lasers," he said. "The things I could do in origami—if I didn't do them, they wouldn't get done."

Lang was right, but there was a hidden meaning in his message. He realized that origami could help a world desperate for solutions. Lang's breakthroughs demonstrated how creative folding techniques can solve a range of mechanical engineering problems. When NASA needed a revolutionary way to fold a telescope into a rocket ship, they availed themselves of Lang's expertise. When a German automaker needed a superior technique to pack air bags, Lang's origami came to the rescue. Today, bioengineers even use his origami approach to pack strands of DNA.

"Almost all innovation happens by making connections between fields that other people don't realize," Lang explained to me. To find opportunity, he said, one should "Look for connections and try to understand the patterns. It's all well and good to see a connection between two fields, but if you understand the underlying pattern, then you can more easily see similar types of connections at play in other fields of endeavor."

Lang's seemingly miraculous ability to expand origami beyond its original roots is an apt metaphor for this book. Lang teaches us that somewhere out there, your big idea probably exists. You just need to know where to look. By learning to find patterns in all sorts of unusual places, you can benefit from advances in other industries, accelerate your search for new ideas, and better realize your potential.

But there's a catch. Pattern awareness is not as easy as it might first seem. In the 1950s, the average life span of a Fortune 500 company was seventy-five years, similar to that of a human. Today, the

---

1   Susan Orlean, "The Origami Lab," *The New Yorker*, February 19, 2007, http://www.newyorker.com/reporting/2007/02/19/070219fa_fact_orlean?currentPage=2.

number has declined to that of a dog—just fifteen years—and some expect it to plummet to just five years.[2] Companies are failing to adapt. In the last decade, Kodak, Border's, Trump Entertainment, Hostess Foods, and Tower Records have all collapsed, not to mention all the U.S. airlines, banks, and automakers that had to be rescued by multibillion-dollar government bailouts. It's clear that we need to be better at spotting the destructive patterns that regularly roll over us like a tidal wave—but we also need to be better at tucking into the curl of that wave and riding it for all it's worth.

After years of advising hundreds of top brands, ranging from Coca-Cola to IBM to Victoria's Secret, I've learned that the only thing more powerful than an idea is the culture that nourishes it—or that prevents it from taking root. Part of what this book offers is a way to overcome the psychological and cultural traps that cause smart people to overlook opportunity.

THE POWER OF THE CROWD

For years, I searched for my own entrepreneurial idea, but like so many people, I never found one that seemed exactly right. By age twenty-nine, I'd worked as a management consultant, as a head of analytics, as an innovation lead, and, finally, as a director for a bank. I'd made a career out of helping other people find *their* ideas without finding my own. So, one morning in the wee hours, I created an online community called Trend Hunter for people to share business ideas. I hoped that someone somewhere would help me find my inspiration—but when the site exploded in growth, I realized Trend Hunter itself was my opportunity.

2   Steve Denning, "Why Did IBM Survive," *Forbes,* July 10, 2011, http://www
.forbes.com/sites/stevedenning/2011/07/10/why-did-ibm-survive.

THE RESEARCH LEADING TO THIS BOOK

At first glance, you might mistake the Trend Hunter site for a media publication, but behind the scenes, it's carefully structured to be a giant research lab. Imagine having six basketball stadiums full of experts to hunt ideas for you. Then imagine testing the appeal of an idea with thousands or in some cases hundreds of thousands of people. That's Trend Hunter. To date, we've analyzed a quarter million products.

Traditionally, trend research had always been dominated by gurus and gut instinct. Our approach departed from that by pooling many people's contributions simultaneously. In 2007, a year before the market crash, we were simultaneously tracking a decline in the love for luxury, a rise in what we dubbed "credit crunch couture," and a "return to the kitchen," three key changes in customer behavior that foretold a market for new products and services. The year before, in 2006, we'd predicted that marketers would shift their budgets from TV to online, and by 2007, we were talking up Twitter as a powerful new marketing platform, even though it had been in existence for only a few months. Again and again, Trend Hunter has proved its efficacy as a global idea engine. It is not hampered by any one person's limitations; rather, it derives surprising predictive power from the input of millions of relentlessly curious people.

When we began offering companies dedicated Trend Hunter researchers, our client list exploded, granting us rare insight into some of the toughest innovation problems businesses face. On any given day, we may be predicting future interfaces for Samsung or Intel, helping Adidas tap into pop culture for its next hit shoe, or inspiring Crayola's creative new toys. These assignments have given us a rare opportunity to battle-test our methodology and learn how the world's brightest innovators stay ahead of the curve.

Along the way, we've interviewed nearly a thousand innovators, entrepreneurs, and clients to better understand their secrets. Drawing from this research, *Better and Faster* will teach you *six* specific patterns that you can use to shortcut your way to opportunity. While the data is deep, my preference is to tell stories—and not just familiar ones, but those you've likely never heard before: tales involving people from every economic stratum who've achieved the incredible. By seeing how specific individuals and companies mastered the patterns, you'll be able to out-innovate, outsmart, and out-maneuver.

Enjoy!

Part I

Awaken

Chapter 1

THE HUNTER AND THE FARMER

Living in an era of unprecedented change, it's easy to think of our potential opportunities as boundless. But there's a catch. We must be smart enough—*evolved* enough—to leverage change. We must get beyond our "farmer" roots and find our inner "hunter."

Ten thousand years ago, something changed. Someone planted the first seeds, ushering in a new era. Humankind had a reliable source of food, eliminating the time-consuming need to seek out wild plants and hunt animals nomadically. People could stay put, build communities, and acquire possessions. Over the next five hundred generations, predictability and protecting order became paramount. We evolved into excellent farmers. It's this simple: Once we find a field to farm, we're neurologically wired to repeat the chain of decisions that led to the last harvest. Today, you can see this wiring in the way most corporations behave. Once a company becomes successful, it creates rules, procedures, and policies to protect the status quo.

Everyone farms. Your "field" might be your job, your product, or your brand, but reflexively, when you find a fertile field, you farm. Your neurological preferences take over and you become protective of your craft, digging in for what you hope will be a repeat of the prior harvest.

While this tendency served us well for the last ten thousand years, it leaves us unprepared for today's era of rapid change. To break free, we need to better understand our farming bias and learn how to awaken our inner hunter. Yes, it's tempting to think, "But I'm *already* a hunter. That's why I'm reading this book. Why can't I just hear about those patterns and get going already!" But there's immense danger in that impatience. If you fall into the traps of the farmer, you won't be able to fully exploit the patterns. So listen up.

THE FARMER: COUGH SYRUP, AWKWARD MOMENTS, AND SEX APPEAL

Roy Raymond was a 1970s version of today's ambitious California entrepreneurs. He was a Stanford business grad on the lookout for a commercial concept he could call his own, and he wasn't finding it pursuing a career at Vicks, the over-the-counter cough syrup company. One day, on a mission to find a gift for his wife, he entered the intimate apparel section of a local department store. The experience was awkward, to say the least. He felt like "an unwelcome intruder," embarrassed and lost in "racks of terry-cloth robes and ugly, floral-print nylon nightgowns."[1]

The discomfort led to an idea: Why not create a guy-friendly shop in which men could buy lingerie for their girlfriends or wives? His idea was rooted in two insights: first, that a lingerie shop geared toward men would make them more comfortable shopping, and second, that truly sexy lingerie would be a hit with both men *and* women.

In 1977, Raymond begged and borrowed $80,000 from his relatives to launch a little lingerie shop. With its wood-paneled walls, fashionable clothing, and upscale, male-oriented theme, the shop racked up sales of half a million dollars in its first year. That success funded three more locations. Aiming to go national, Raymond launched a mail-order catalog that was the talk of the industry and won additional notice when it was pinned up in men's locker rooms

---

1   Emily Newhall, "A Catalog-Business Boom," *Newsweek,* November 16, 1981.

everywhere. Within a few years, he was adding new locations and reaping millions in revenue.

By now, you've probably guessed that Raymond's store was Victoria's Secret, although little remains of Raymond's business model in the international chain we know today. Raymond did many things correctly, including transforming a broken shopping experience into a lucrative retail concept and exploiting an untapped niche, for which he reaped the rewards. But, despite those smart moves, he didn't see the bigger picture. It turned out, of course, that *women* buy most lingerie, not men—so Raymond was marketing to the wrong sex. Indeed, the main reason that women shopped at his stores was the fashionable lingerie, but not specifically because it made men happy. Rather, because it made women feel more confident. Raymond missed all that, and eventually his chain was headed for bankruptcy. That's when retailing magnate Leslie Wexner took the enterprise off his hands.

Within months, the new managers radically repositioned the stores and catalogue: imagery, brand, colors, and styles were all redesigned for a woman's eye, and the fresh, female-empowering approach worked like a charm. The result: Three decades later, Victoria's Secret has grown into a $6 billion megabrand.

It would be easy to dismiss Raymond's talents based on the scale of his blunder. You might argue that he was overlooking the obvious, but don't forget that his initial stores made millions. He had a proven formula, and he stuck by it for years.

Unfortunately, like many individuals and teams, Raymond was only too happy to play the role of the farmer. Had he experimented more and been willing to cast aside his strongly held beliefs, he might have taken full advantage of the tremendous opportunities his company was poised to exploit.

What opportunities are *you* missing right now? How many breakthrough business ideas are just a few steps away from what you're already working on? The reality is that you can't know. Unlike

Raymond, most of us will never see someone else come and do our job so much better.

While Raymond's failure was catastrophic, his shortcomings are common among businesses and entrepreneurs. Raymond suffered from the three farmer traps: He was complacent with his own success, repetitive, and overly protective of his own beliefs.

As strange as it may sound, one of the hard-to-fathom lessons from these traps is that "being good" at something may eventually keep you from reaching your full potential.

THE HUNTER: COUTURE, BLUE JEANS, AND NO PHOTOGRAPHS

To understand how to skirt these common traps, let's meet an unlikely hunter, a seventy-eight-year-old man who lives in the bustling Spanish port city of A Coruña. He wears the same blue outfit nearly every day. He eats lunch in his work cafeteria and rarely goes on vacation. He doesn't do interviews. In fact, until 1999, no published photograph existed of this mysterious man.

Indeed, the only reason he finally deigned to be photographed at all was that he *had* to as part of his company's initial public offering. He earned his billions by revolutionizing fashion, and today, he's the world's third-wealthiest individual, richer than Warren Buffet and Larry Ellison, and just behind Carlos Slim and Bill Gates.

Amancio Ortega is the creator of Zara, a thriving international chain of clothing stores that you might mistakenly think is like any other, except that it's completely different. Louis Vuitton's fashion director calls Zara "possibly the most innovative and devastating retailer in the world."[2] The company doesn't advertise because it can't and doesn't need to. Zara doesn't carry every design and size

---

2 "Zara, a Spanish Success Story," CNN, June 15, 2001, http://edition.cnn.com/BUSINESS/programs/yourbusiness/stories2001/zara.

in stock, and styles are rarely consistent. And that's precisely why it succeeds.

To understand how Zara has made Ortega fabulously wealthy is to understand the future of business—in *any* industry. This is not a lesson in fashion.

It starts with speed. An average clothing company takes several months or up to a year to turn a design into a product ready for purchase. Zara takes just fourteen days.[3]

Designers and pattern makers craft several concepts throughout each day, which the company speedily manufactures from its local factory. Outsourcing to China is not an option, because distance would delay production. Zara often starts by working with *greige* textiles, meaning that they are in an unfinished, near-colorless state. Working with textiles in such a state means that they can be dyed at the last minute.

If Zara's latest inspiration is a little red dress with a collar, five sizes of that design will be crafted and shipped to each of Zara's 2,000 stores—all within two weeks. Buy that red dress and a sales-clerk will ask why you like it. Such questions might seem innocuous, but at the end of the day, the legions of storekeepers report back to the head office. If enough women like the dress but aren't crazy about the collar, the designer will bang out a fresh collar-free design, and in fourteen days, it will hit all 2,000 stores.

Slim inventory has multiple benefits. The company is seldom stuck with clothing it can't sell, and advertising is unnecessary, irrelevant, and impossible because there's no logic in putting a dress on a billboard if it won't be available next week. And finally, the limited supply reinforces exclusivity. If you're lucky enough to snare this week's hot new skirt, great, but if you hesitate, it may never be

---

3   "The Reclusive Billionaire: Secret Life of Zara Boss Amancio Ortega and His 'Fast Fashion' Empire," *The Age*, March 5, 2013, http://www.theage.com.au/ executive-style/management/the-reclusive-billionaire-secret-life-of-zara-boss -amancio-ortega-and-his-fast-fashion-empire-20130305-2fhne.html.

in the store again. This sparks urgency, tapping into the predator-prey psychology that hooks so many shoppers. Customers also take comfort in knowing that coworkers are unlikely to show up to work in the same dress.

These unusual methods have helped Zara become one of the world's fastest-growing and most disruptive retailers. In an article on the company, the British newspaper *The Telegraph* reported that the opening of a Zara store is the "signifier of a stylish city," and it quoted one young woman as saying, "Thank God, we won't be a third-world fashion country any more."[4]

Unlike the "farmer" archetype I've described, Ortega is not complacent. He is insatiable. In his words, whether you're a designer or a storekeeper, "the daily task is marked by self-improvement and the search for new opportunity." Ortega doesn't lapse into repetition. Nor is he protective of his fashionable designs. He is relentlessly curious and willing to destroy.

These are the three hunter instincts—insatiability, curiosity, and willingness to destroy.

AWAKENING YOUR INNER HUNTER

While these may sound like simple concepts, putting them into practice is another matter. The first step is to awaken, a process that I was reminded of during a pre-event phone call for a corporate keynote. The company CEO pumped me up Tony Robbins style, despite the fact that I was the one hired to deliver the motivational talk.

He heads a multibillion-dollar insurance company that is grow-

---

4   Marion Hume, "The Secrets of Zara's Success," *Telegraph* (London), June 22, 2011, http://fashion.telegraph.co.uk/news-features/TMG8589217/The-secrets-of-Zaras-success.html.

ing, though not as fast as his shareholders might like. He wasted no time: "Can I be candid with you? Can we just talk like we're a couple girls hanging out in a locker room?" I thought, "Well, I don't get that reference . . . but sure."

He continued with a salty diatribe that ramped up like a speech delivered by a tough football coach whose team is down at half-time. "Our brand is like a lion. We grew up kings. We claimed our land. But now we're that same big lion and we're sleeping under a tree. People come to work, earn their keep, pay the mortgage, and go home. We're good, but not great. We've lost our hunger. We're a lion sitting under the tree, watching the hyenas as they stalk our territory. They're coming right up to us. They scratch. They push. They're eating our food! At a certain point, we need to remember that we're a f***ing lion. We need to stand up, and we need to f***ing roar!"

Complacency was the enemy of this hunter, and he was more than aware of it—he was *obsessed*. "Things need to change," the CEO growled, "and they need to change now. People are either with me in the new world order, or they're not. And that might mean that not everyone is right for the job anymore. It might mean that the people change. But one thing is certain," he thundered. "We are hunters, and now is our time to hunt!"

Many of today's mightiest companies are great lions. They have the ability to claim new territory fiercely, but once they do, they're often tempted to take a break and bask in their glory. Kings of the jungle, they can't imagine being dethroned. That attitude doesn't go unnoticed. The rest of the animal kingdom picks up on this complacency. They smell it and know it. The hyenas become a little more daring and hungry.

Confronted with a business world no longer defined by stability and predictability, you need to adapt. It's time to step out of the shadows of your predecessors—time to sharpen your weapons.

Hunters look for clues, listen for footsteps, and scan for the scents that lead to opportunity. If your spear misses its target, throw another or fashion a better weapon. Hunters constantly reassess signals and seek new patterns that will help them track their next prey.

Now is the time to awaken your inner hunter. Dart in. Feast as the lion dozes! Create a culture of speed and recognize that your key advantage is the ability to understand your customer, adapt, and fashion fast solutions.

It doesn't matter how big you are. Stand up, claim what's yours, and roar.

Chapter 2

FARMER TRAPS VS. HUNTER INSTINCTS

Awakening your inner hunter, as I've discussed, requires you to better understand farmer traps. It also requires you to develop instincts to avoid those traps.

FARMER TRAP #1: COMPLACENCY

Thirty years ago, baby boomers launched their blue-chip careers confident that their large, stable employers would steadily increase their salaries for the rest of their working days. That world is gone. Today, even well-managed companies fail to adapt, largely because of the complacency that so often insidiously worms itself into a firm's culture.

In my first book, *Exploiting Chaos,* I wrote of an iconic, game-changing company that reinvented communication. Innovation was in the company's blood: It invented the spell checker, grammar checker, and laptop word-processor. In 1989, the company hauled in half a billion dollars in revenue and was still growing. Most people would guess that I'm referring to Apple, Microsoft, HP, IBM, or Xerox, but those aren't even close. The company was Smith Corona, the best typewriter company in the world.

Smith Corona did dabble in computing in a 1990 joint venture with Acer. But less than two years later, Smith Corona's CEO abruptly canceled the foray, noting, "Many people believe that the typewriter and word-processor business is a buggy-whip industry, which is far from true. There is still a strong market for our products in the United States and the world."[1]

The CEO's foolish choice of words, horrible timing, and lack of foresight were extraordinary. Three years later, Smith Corona declared bankruptcy, and Acer went on to become, at one point, the world's second-largest PC company.

Smith Corona is not alone. Over the decades, many once-dominant corporations have fallen from grace. For example, there was a time when corporate yuppies gleefully bragged about their BlackBerry addictions. To maintain its leading position, Black-Berry (originally called Research in Motion) built a strong business brand that boasted unparalleled security and reliability. These qualities provided the company with the equivalent of a medieval castle's moat, blocking competitors from entering the corporate market. But BlackBerry's inward focus and complacency blinded the company to the potential of the rapidly expanding consumer market. And that nearsightedness spelled its doom. Mainstream non–business consumers rushed to stylish offerings from Apple and Samsung. Gradually, the upstarts also improved their security and reliability and ate away at BlackBerry's beloved corporate market. It was the knockout punch Blackberry didn't see coming, sending it into a vicious downward spiral.

At a corporate level, it's easy to see how complacency can happen. But the trap ensnares individuals, too. All too often, people shape their careers around superficial, short-term goals, only to find themselves cramped by improper incentives and rigid structures. For example, a recent ESPN documentary titled *Broke* revealed that 78 percent of NFL players are bankrupt (or near bankrupt) within a

---

1   Kris Frieswick, "The Turning Point," *CFO Magazine*, April 1, 2005, http://ww2
.cfo.com/strategy/2005/04/the-turning-point.

few years of retirement, and 60 percent of NBA retirees follow the same path. Similar spectacular rises and falls plague movie stars, rappers, small-business owners, and venture-capital-funded entrepreneurs. It's a pattern repeated by millions and highlights a deeper problem relating to people's ability to handle change.

Consider the rise and fall of M.C. Hammer, one of the biggest successes and failures in the history of rap. Those who glance superficially at his story might assume that he was a one-hit wonder of limited drive and talent. Actually, Hammer worked incredibly hard. After three years in the navy, he didn't just sign to a label, he started his own, knowing that record labels often rake in more money than individual artists. In the early days, he promoted relentlessly, selling records from the trunk of his car. And although most people stopped tuning in after his 1991 megahit *Too Legit to Quit,* he kept recording, releasing eight more albums.

But at the peak of his earning power, Hammer made a colossal miscalculation. He spent far more than he could possibly earn—at one point, he was blowing roughly half a million a month on his entourage—and then his popularity plummeted. His aptly named hit "U Can't Touch This" was itself a 1989 metaphor for being on the top of his game. But good times don't last forever, and like so many rappers who'd risen and fallen before him, Hammer was destined for a hard crash. By 1996, his $33 million fortune was spent, he filed for bankruptcy, and Hammer Time was history.

Seemingly borrowing a page from the M.C. Hammer playbook, countless businesses fail to adapt and foolishly squander marketing and innovation dollars. And this occurs even more dramatically with companies that have experienced success. Success breeds a form of complacency in which workers fall into the trap of "playing with the house's money." The phrase has its roots in the fact that gamblers take on too much risk after a big win, gambling their newly won money as if it still belonged to the casino (known as "the house").

HUNTER INSTINCT #1: INSATIABILITY

To counteract complacency, you must exhibit insatiability. Eat or be eaten—that's the primal force that drives the hunter. While hunters may enjoy the occasional feast, far more often they must scan the horizon for their next meal. It helps if hunters exist in a culture that is obsessed with pleasing the customer.

Richard Fairbank is the Amancio Ortega of the credit card industry. Like Ortega, he's wealthy and reclusive, and he's not someone whom most people would know of or recognize. Yet Fairbank is the founder of the remarkably successful bank Capital One.

Back in 2006, Capital One began running a series of hit commercials featuring "Visigoth" bankers. The point was that if a band of barbaric bankers were preparing to pillage your savings, you'd sure want someone on your side. The metaphor was meant to symbolize the difference between "old school" banks and Capital One.

By 2014, nearly fifty million people had a Capital One card in their wallet. Before Capital One, almost every credit card had a 20 percent rate and an annual fee. It was a "one size fits all" financial world dominated by incumbent banks. Fairbank's belief was that an insatiable focus on data and analytics—much like Ortega's penchant for tracking fashion trends—could lead to something much different. If you understood everything about your customers, you could better predict their product usage, likelihood to repay loans, and general interests. That would allow you to deliver personalized rates, fees, and perks in a way that no other bank could match.

Way back in 1999, when most competitors lacked a website, *Fast Company* wrote about Fairbank's insatiability: When a customer dials in, "high-speed computers swing into action. Loaded with background information on one in seven U.S. households and with exhaustive data about how the company's millions of customers behave, the computers identify who is calling and predict the reason for the call. After reviewing fifty options for whom to notify, the computers pick the best option for each situation. The computers also pull and pass along about two dozen pieces of information about the person who is calling. They even predict what the caller might want to buy."[2]

By then, the eleven-year-old Capital One had amassed 16.7 million customers and an archive of 28,000 financial experiments—each a novel combination of product, price, and promotion. Fairbank told *Fast Company* that his success was driven by a much broader hunger for innovation: "Credit cards aren't banking—they're information," he explained. "What we've done is to create an innovation machine." In the following decade, Capital One smartly expanded beyond cards into mortgages, small business, and retail banking, tripling its customer base to 45 million.

I began working at Capital One Canada in 2004. We'd test several products each month, including impossible combinations that could never be profitable. But maybe, just maybe, something else would make that product profitable in the future, and prior testing would prove valuable.

Three years in, our appetite for testing had increased. My team led the way with some of the company's first design of experiments (DOE) testing. To get a sense of DOE, imagine that you're designing a vehicle. You can choose to design a car, truck, boat, or motorbike. The vehicle can be fast, stylish, or economical. Red, blue, black, white, gray, or yellow. Powered by diesel, gasoline, or battery. Finally, it can also sport the brand name Super, Awesome, Cool, Affordable, or Elegant. Taken together, those add up to many choices—1,080 combinations, to be exact. Far too many to test. But with some bad-ass math, you can actually predict the best combinations by testing twenty or thirty random combinations.

---

2   Charles Fishman, "This Is a Marketing Revolution," *Fast Company*, May 1999, http://www.fastcompany.com/36975/marketing-revolution.

To accelerate Capital One's ability to evolve and change, Fairbank bred a culture in which people and roles were constantly adapting. Destroying archaic company structures is the fastest path to that goal. Fairbank put experimenting ahead of hierarchy. For example, if a junior staffer had an idea for a clever but counterintuitive test, we wouldn't overrule him or her. We'd simply add that person's test to the next experiment. If it worked, that junior analyst would take a day to celebrate—then immediately dive into another experiment. The system was constantly evolving.

In my case, I began in the valuations team. When my prediction models outperformed past approaches, I was quickly promoted to run that team. But I yearned for something more, so I wrote a proposal to start a "Competitive Strategy and Innovation Team." I wanted to be part of a cross-functional team that could dream up new products and build a superior pipeline of future products. When I finished presenting the idea, my boss said, "Great, where do I sign up?" I didn't quite understand until he made my real-time promotion clear: "It's your team, so pick the people and start running it."

That opportunity to leapfrog hierarchy rarely happens to twenty-eight-year-olds, especially at a bank. It was a great opportunity, and soon I received another promotion and was running a business line. The catch was that market shifts were pressuring our margins. When I took over, the company gave me a goal of making sure the business didn't shrink more than 20 percent. The assignment was deflating. Imagine crowing to your friends, "My new job is going great! I only shrunk the business by 20 percent."

Fortunately, I never had to have that conversation. Capital One's hunter mentality made it possible for me to test ideas that wouldn't fly at most banks, including a plan to physically meet potential customers. I set up booths across the country, in shopping malls and public squares, and joined my team in sporting Capital One

T-shirts and asking people what they were looking for from a credit card.

By meeting customers, we discovered a much simpler way to describe our new product. It's funny how you can become such an expert that you lose touch with how customers think about your category. For instance, we loved numbers and jargon, but to ordinary people we were just selling another credit card. One of the things I learned along the way is that sometimes you have to un-learn what you think is great. Then you can open yourself up to what your customer is really thinking.

At the time, our key product had a consistent low rate of 5.99 percent—by far the lowest Canadian price. Strangely, it didn't matter. Like bears to honey, consumers were drawn to the low introductory prices of our rivals—even if their cards were deceptive and jumped to 20 percent after a few months. Simple math told us that our product was far better for people over the long term, so this was really frustrating.

Our traditional focus groups and surveys hadn't been helpful. But because we were out meeting customers, we learned something critical. Consumers didn't understand how different we were from the competition. They jumped to an erroneous conclusion—assuming that we started at 5.99 percent and leaped to 20 percent.

Our breakthrough came from my next tests. We priced everything based on the prime rate, just like a mortgage. Instead of 5.99 percent, we marketed Prime+2 and Prime+1 credit cards, and people loved it. The pricing seemed fair and it helped consumers realize that the rate wouldn't skyrocket. By the next month, our new bookings had tripled and the business quickly grew to a one-billion-dollar portfolio of low-risk assets.

That billion-dollar portfolio was my corporate badge of honor, but more important, it taught me a key entrepreneurial lesson: To win long term, you need to be structured to adapt.

I left Capital One in 2007 to take Trend Hunter to the next level. Timing, as they say, is everything, and as it happened, that was just a year before the credit crunch took out 465 American banks,[3] from Washington Mutual (the largest bank failure in U.S. history) to IndyMac, Colonial, Guaranty, BankUnited, AmTrust, California National, and Superior. Needless to say, I kept a close eye on Capital One. Thanks to massive testing and an uncanny ability to adapt, the company emerged unscathed. Not only did it survive, it grew.

No matter what business you're in, to thrive you must fight the presumption that you know your customer. Also, you must push yourself to challenge "certainties." Relentlessly seek out and talk to customers, and don't be afraid to prove yourself wrong. You need to fight your own arrogance and test impossibilities.

FARMER TRAP #2: REPETITION

Each season, the farmer dutifully repeats the same tasks: seeding, tending, watering, and, finally, harvesting. He or she counts on a routine to deliver maximum yield and doesn't dare diverge from that pattern.

Similarly, public companies strive for consistent decision-making and predictable quarterly results. Once they hit a groove, they scale by repeating and optimizing their processes.

David Cook understood this proven business strategy when he launched Blockbuster Video in October of 1985. He was a database specialist, already wealthy from his data-driven days, and his goal was to build a turnkey video rental franchise business. Much of his

---

3 "Failed Bank List," Federal Deposit Insurance Corporation (alternatively: http://en.wikipedia.org/wiki/List_of_bank_failures_in_the_United_States_%282008%E2%80%93present%29#cite_note-FDIC-1).

success was based on using data to predict what consumers might want to watch—not too different from Netflix's strategy today.

Cook's first few stores were hugely successful, so he decided to scale by replicating each store down to the last detail. By 2009, Blockbuster had planted its flag in 9,000 locations and employed roughly 60,000 people.

Ironically, Blockbuster had multiple opportunities over the years to buy upstart Netflix for what in retrospect could only be viewed as a steal. But the retail behemoth didn't see the need, and in 2004, it launched Total Access, its own online DVD rental website. But the website wasn't given much chance to succeed. By 2007, Blockbuster was drastically deemphasizing Total Access, believing it was too detached from its highly successful franchised store model.

What happened after that?

Yes, you guessed it: In the next few years, Blockbuster sank like the *Titanic*. In 2010, the nearly defunct chain was overrun by streamed video delivery. Blockbuster declared bankruptcy, and Netflix skyrocketed into a $26 billion company.

Optimization is a seductive tool. It tempts CEOs and managers to drive down a broad, seemingly guaranteed highway to a conservative outcome instead of striking out on a narrow path to a possibly outrageous hit. Companies love to roll out policies, procedures, hierarchy, and guidelines to scale a business, but inevitably the rigid structure limits flexibility and hampers their ability to adapt.

As individuals, we, too, can easily blunder into the trap of repetition. Once you find an industry that pays well, you'll tend to stick with it. Hit on a new investment category that delivers profits, and you'll be tempted to overinvest in that niche. And once you enjoy career success, you'll likely repeat what got you there in the first place, missing some of the best new opportunities to come along.

HUNTER INSTINCT #2: CURIOSITY

Breaking free from repetition requires sharpening your hunter's instinct for curiosity. To inspire curiosity in your organization, it's essential to seek out fresh sources and experiment with new ideas constantly.

Born and raised in rough-and-tumble South Central Los Angeles, Ron Finley is an African American entrepreneur famous for donning tailor-fitted denim suits—tangible proof of how he beat the odds through his rebellious style of entrepreneurism. Despite growing up in one of America's most dangerous neighborhoods, Finley rose to become a successful fashion designer, collector, and, more recently, a leading force in transforming his community.

The violence and gang activity of South Central is known to many, but the region is also the cultural heartbeat of California's black community and the birthplace of stars ranging from Barry White to Ice Cube. As a young man who was curious about his culture, Finley progressed from collecting 1930s swimsuits, old watches, and cameras to focusing on black entertainment memorabilia. In fact, he would develop a collection so impressive that it would eventually be displayed at the Museum of African American Art.

Finley's curiosity was matched by a healthy rebellious streak. When he was a high school student, teachers informed him that home economics classes were for girls, but he countered that most chefs are men and that he wanted to learn to cook. And just like that, his high school permitted boys to take home economics.

Once Finley had exhausted his curiosity about food, he turned to clothing. He wondered why fashion designers never made anything for the people from *his* neighborhood. So in his family's small garage, he started sewing custom-tailored hoodies, denim coats, and sleek blazers that soon caught on with celebrities, rappers, and NBA stars, from Will Smith to Shaquille O'Neal to Robert Horry.

Finley's Dropdead Collexion became a top seller at Neiman Marcus, Nordstrom, and Saks Fifth Avenue.

But Finley didn't ditch South Central, jump into a limo, motor on over to Beverly Hills, and never look back. Why didn't he abandon such a crime-ridden neighborhood? Quite simply, he was still feeding his curiosity in South Central.

As he looked around, he started noticing the surging rise in "liquor stores, fast food and vacant lots." The clues all pointed to an abundance of unhealthy food. He told me that he was seeing "more and more overweight children," a dramatic rise in dialysis clinics, and parking lots full of motorized scooters for the obese. But nobody else seemed to be noticing. If they did, they certainly weren't doing anything about it.

As Finley expanded his research, he stumbled on the concept of a food desert, the term for a lower-income district that lacks access to fresh food. Food deserts are largely an American phenomenon affecting tens of millions. Finley realized South Central L.A. had become one of those deserts.

He learned that South Los Angeles is plagued with five times the obesity rate of nearby ultra-rich Beverly Hills. "Imagine if your neighborhood was devoid of any kind of real food," he told me. "What if everything was fast food or highly processed? What if you couldn't buy an apple?"

Finley decided he would attack the problem. He didn't know how to garden, but the hunter in him saw potential in all the vacant lots and city-owned strips of land next to every sidewalk. He enrolled in a course, bought some tools, and uprooted the city-owned grass next to his sidewalk to plant his first seeds.

He wasn't sure what would happen, and for a couple of weeks his guerilla garden looked like just another slot of vacant dirt. Then Finley's first vegetables sprouted—arugula, onions, garlic, and carrots. He saw the vegetables as a metaphor. "Growing your own money," he called it.

Inquisitive neighbors began asking Finley about the mysterious pop-up crops sprouting in South Los Angeles. When kids came to check out his garden, he began envisioning how urban gardening might become a tool of rehabilitation. He dreamed of teaching others to garden so that the food desert he found himself in the midst of would become transformed into a food forest.

Late one night, Finley spotted a mother and her daughter in his yard picking vegetables. He came out and told them that the food was for them—for the taking. "People asked me, 'Fin, aren't you afraid people are going to steal your food?' And I'm like, 'Hell no, I ain't afraid they're going to steal it. That's why it's on the street!'"[4]

Then someone complained. It seemed Finley was breaking the rules: You can't appropriate land from the city and turn it into a vegetable garden. Finley saw "the heat" as a chance to take his cause to the next level. He brought his crusade to the *Los Angeles Times* and his city councilor, and he circulated a change.org petition that inspired signatures from 900 supporters.

Today, Finley is credited as being one of the founders of LA GreenGrounds, a diverse group of renegade gardeners—many of them ex–gang members—that is growing hundreds of edible plant variations on vacant lots.

Finley teaches us to connect the dots. He shows us that maintaining constant awareness of your surroundings can lead to deciphering meaningful patterns. He also demonstrates that if you remove your blinders and look at the things and people in the background, not just the main characters, you can explore new worlds and transition to a new career more easily than you might think. To do it, you just need to pull the trigger and follow your curiosity.

---

4   Ron Finley, interview by Guy Raz, December 20, 2013, transcript, "How Can You Give a Community Better Health?," Jefferson Public Radio, http://ijpr.org/post/how-can-you-give-community-better-health.

COVER MODELS, LOVE LETTERS, AND MAGNETIC BALLS

"Dear Stranger, you look fantastic in that coat. Someone had to say it, and that someone might as well be me."

You might think that "love letter" a little odd, but you also might smile if a stranger handed it to you in Starbucks, simply to brighten your day. On a whim, Jake Bronstein and his girlfriend wrote and delivered 1,000 similarly worded love notes to delight strangers. Why? It was one of Bronstein's experiments in fun.

I'd been a fan of Bronstein's stunts and quirky endeavors long before we finally met in a Manhattan pub. Sporting oversized 1960s glasses, a plaid shirt, and a hoodie, Bronstein has the aura of a quintessential hipster riding the subway with his skateboard in one hand and an *FHM* magazine in the other. And there's good reason for that, as he was one of the founding editors of the popular men's magazine.

During his tenure, *FHM* became *Adweek*'s fastest-growing U.S. men's magazine. Bronstein is credited with some of the magazine's hit stories and photos, but after six years of editing articles about beer pong, Bronstein saw his tenure at *FHM* come to an ironic but abrupt end. Why? Some innocuous remarks about Howard Stern's girlfriend in a radio interview got him fired.

Needing a new direction and forced to take personal inventory, Bronstein recognized that curiosity and fun were common themes in his life.

The journey he set off on wasn't typical for someone in search of a new job or business. He set up a website, Zoomdoggle, that would launch him on dozens upon dozens of creative experiments. After several hundred, each crazier than the last, Bronstein found himself contemplating a genuinely fresh idea—magnetic neodymium balls. The pea-sized little balls cling together and can be formed into interesting shapes. They were originally designed for the practical but dull purpose of helping researchers study molecular geometry. Grab a handful of these little magnets, however, and you'll have a tough time putting them down. Soon, Bronstein and his buddy, Craig Zucker, wondered if they could become a hot new geeky office toy. "The first (and biggest) questions that needed answering," Bronstein told me, were the extremely simple but incredibly important ones: "What are they for? What do people do with them?" The answers to these questions turned out to be similar to the purpose of George and Seinfeld's show "about nothing."

They called their product Buckyballs, and they packaged the magnetic balls in a funky box marked with the words "no instructions." During the next two thrilling years, Bronstein and Zucker sold more than 3 million packages, generating an estimated $50 million in revenue.

Then came chaos. In July of 2012, the Consumer Product Safety Commission requested that Buckyballs stop selling the product because they believed there was a risk that young children might swallow the balls. This eventually led Bronstein and Zucker to shut down production and recall the product.

Now Bronstein was back to square one—again.

While looking for a new idea, he found himself checking out an American Apparel ad. He thought about the value of the "Made in America" slogan. But he also recognized that American Apparel had been plagued by controversy, international bans, and allegations that its advertising oversexualizes young women. Despite Bronstein's own racy *FHM* background, he dreamed of launching a more wholesomely branded American clothing company.

Few novices have the audacity to think they can launch a clothing company, but to Bronstein, this was just another experiment. He found an American-based factory that could manufacture his first product, boxer shorts, and he created a website for a brand he called Flint and Tinder.

He then launched his Kickstarter. His goal: pre-sell $30,000 of the high-quality boxers. Instead, he pre-sold $291,493—at the time, the most successful Kickstarter campaign ever. Next up, he pre-sold over one million dollars in hoodies—another record.

Bronstein teaches us that play should be encouraged and that success comes from pursuing curiosity and experimentation relentlessly. Also, importantly, he tested his business idea in small steps, like that Kickstarter campaign aimed at seeing if there was a market for his product. Today, it's never been easier to produce prototypes, to market ideas, and to test business concepts without the hassle and risk of a big capital outlay.

PRINCESS, MODEL, ENTREPRENEUR: TRIPLE THREAT

In the early 1960s, Diane Halfin was a determined young woman studying economics at the University of Geneva. She was on track for a predictable and potentially bland career in economics, but she was curious about fashion. As you might guess, job openings for fashion economists are few and far between. Intent on following her passion, she left Switzerland—and the potential of high-paying work—to pursue an internship as a photographer's assistant in Paris. "I didn't know what I wanted to do," she said. "But I always knew the woman I wanted to be."

Next, she landed an apprenticeship in Italy with renowned designer Angelo Ferretti. The job paid just a fraction of what she might have earned as an economist, but she learned how to design her own attire. Her ambition stemmed from her mother, a Holocaust survivor who taught her fear was never an option.

On her journey of self-discovery, she fell in love, but not with just any man—rather, with a prince. She became Her Highness Princess Diane von Furstenberg, better known today by her brand: DVF. Like most royalty, Princess von Furstenberg didn't have to work, but she never lost her longing to build a fashion brand. She continued designing her own line, sending out photos of her designs with herself as the model. Princess, model, and entrepreneur—von Furstenberg was a triple threat.

Although she divorced her prince in 1972, her interpretation of the wrap dress, one of her more creative designs, caught the eye of Diana Vreeland, the famed *Vogue* editor. And, when Vreeland called von Furstenberg's work "absolutely smashing," the company's annual sales quickly skyrocketed to $150 million. Curiosity paid off.

To my delight, Diane von Furstenberg recently sent Trend Hunter a note saying that she was a fan and wanted to meet. On the night that I interviewed her, she was celebrating a successful runway show and a new type of social shopping technology in her New York City concept store. I asked how she stays on the cutting edge, expecting to hear that she pores over fashion magazines and frequents the major fashion shows. But instead she said, "I always carry around a camera. You never know what you'll see. When I spot a young woman with an attractive or unusual outfit, maybe a combination I've never seen before, I ask to photograph her."

To fuel her curiosity, she lives and works out of the same four-story brick building in New York City's meatpacking district. You might expect her to live in a glamorous apartment in New York's Upper East Side or in Paris, but she finds those places boring. She lives and works in the same building to stay connected to her customers and to her experiments. The store itself is another by-product of her curiosity. She was one of the first shopkeepers to colonize New York's meatpacking district—way back in the 1970s when the area was seedy and dangerous. Today, it has become a mecca for North American fashion designers.

As for technology, she partnered with HP because she wanted to fulfill dreams she had about social shopping. While her competitors were still figuring out whether they should start a Twitter account, von Furstenberg had installed interactive touch screens throughout her store. The screens allow customers to mix and match outfits and accessories and share their picks with friends before deciding on their purchase.

DVF teaches us to invest time and effort in understanding our new market, even if it means accepting a job with lesser pay. She shows us to explore the world like a curious child, open the potential of what could be.

FARMER TRAP #3: PROTECTIVENESS

The inherently protective perspective of the farmer often has him or her erecting barriers to protect the status quo. But when the world changes swiftly, that conservatism inhibits evolution. Grasping at what worked in the past becomes counterproductive.

Consider the cautionary tale of Steven Sasson, a brilliant young scientist whose curiosity led him to invent the digital camera. The catch is that he invented the camera four decades ago for Kodak, a lumbering monopolist that blew the chance to exploit his invention.

In 1976, Sasson banged out a report for Kodak titled "The Camera of the Future." The report predicted memory cards, image storing, and a process for zipping images over phone lines—quite forward-looking given the decade. Sasson was an electrical engineer who explained to me that he thought "it would be neat to make a camera with no moving parts." With a small budget, he built a working prototype.

His digital camera attracted much attention inside Kodak, but senior management countered with a host of reasons why it wouldn't catch on. "They thought people wouldn't want to watch pictures on a TV set," he told me. They said, "Prints look better!" And that observation would block Kodak from realizing the potential of his innovation.

Kodak was obsessed with the perfect picture. "The image-quality issue was a cultural thing. Culture plays a big part in any innovation process," he told me. "Our culture was to provide the best possible images. Film had enormous capability. The argument was: Would the imaging [of digital] ever reach the quality necessary to meet [the quality of] film?"

When it came to film, Kodak "could control most aspects of the imaging chain." They sold the chemicals, the film, and the paper, and ultimately, they could guarantee near-perfect photos and prints.

Decades later, the film giant was pressed into making a last-ditch investment when its fierce film rival, Fuji, entered digital photography. This belated competition spurred Kodak to develop dozens of new digital technologies. But it was too little too late. The company had spent too many decades protecting its "perfect" film business, and in 2012, Kodak declared bankruptcy.

Today, Sasson sounds haunted by the reality that he might have been the Henry Ford of digital photography if only Kodak had been more aggressive. "I keep thinking of the culture. Kodak had a good culture. But I do believe that every strong culture contains the seed of its own destruction. A culture is a defined set of behaviors that develop over time. But when new opportunities arise, the culture holds you back."

Kodak isn't alone. In the 1980s, Microsoft, which wanted to transform how people learn, approached Britannica with the prospect of turning its respected encyclopedia content into a CD-ROM. But Britannica was a successful brand with a near-monopoly. They immediately turned down the offer, publicly declaring, "The Encyclopedia Britannica has no plans to be on a home computer. And since the market is so small, only 4 to 5 percent of households have computers, we would not want to hurt our traditional way of selling."[5]

Boy, did they ever misjudge the future.

Undaunted, Microsoft purchased a weaker competitor, Funk

---

5   Shane Greenstein and Michelle Devereux, "Crisis at Encyclopedia Britannica," Kellogg School of Management, http://www.slideshare.net/renerojas/case-study -encyclopedia-britannica.

& Wagnall's Encyclopedia, and quickly turned it into Microsoft Encarta. Within a few years, Microsoft's CD-ROM encyclopedia became the most commercially successful encyclopedia of all time. Now it was Microsoft that was the near-monopolist—the hunter had captured its quarry. But as so often happens, this, too, bred complacency. Much as Britannica had rejected sharing its content on the PC, Microsoft, to protect its CD-ROM sales, declined to share Encarta on the Internet. This set the stage for Wikipedia's sweeping in with a divergent new encyclopedia model (one that enlisted amateurs to contribute entries), and Wikipedia very quickly became the sixth most popular website. Just like that, Encarta was as behind the times as Britannica's hardbound encyclopedia.

Success can blind us. Though Bill Gates earned tens of billions in the fast-moving world of high-tech, even he recognized Microsoft's many failures in exploiting new markets. In his book *The Road Ahead*, he wrote, "Success is a lousy teacher. It seduces smart people into thinking they can't lose. And it's an unreliable guide to the future."[6]

Kodak and Microsoft were masters of their markets, but each mistakenly behaved like a farmer, protecting their territory and missing out on what would become the breakthrough product.

On an individual level, these traps cause people to hang on to past success, cling to one career too long, and resist trying new technologies and different ways of getting work done.

Once we become successful, we tend to fall into the strategy of losing sports teams: trying to protect a lead. Skirting risk and seeking perfection sound like great goals, but unfortunately perfection takes too long and can be elusive. Today you must retool your innovation process for speed. You must move fast and fix later.

You must embrace the third and final hunter instinct.

---

6   Bill Gates, Nathan Myhrvold, Peter Rinearson, *The Road Ahead*. New York: Penguin Books, 1996.

HUNTER INSTINCT #3: WILLINGNESS TO DESTROY

To avoid falling into the trap of protectiveness, you need to be willing to destroy—that is, to abandon the relative safety of normalcy. The hunter must be able to scrap his or her current plans and try something bold.

At twenty-nine, Eric Ripert became one of the youngest chefs to receive four stars from the *New York Times*. He would become the first chef to be so honored five consecutive times. He's also one of the few to earn three Michelin stars, the "Academy Award" of the culinary arts.[7] Nearly a decade later, his hair is streaked with silver, but his cooking talents remain supreme. Unlike so many chefs who've risen and fallen, he still has all of those Michelin stars, which are far easier to earn than to hold on to. The *New York Times* summed up the challenge that confronts any master chef:

> There is reason to pity the nearly perfect. They have so many ways to falter. In thrall to their own legend, they might well overreach, trading glory for folly, or they might simply coast, converting acclaim into idle narcissism. They might allow self-assurance to bleed into arrogance and let down their guard against error.[8]

Why is it so tough for a chef to maintain a culinary throne? You can tantalize taste buds and impress the critics, rocketing to fame for one season, but by the following year, you're expected to induce jaw-dropping, mouthwatering meals with an entirely re-vamped menu. Repeating past success with a new product each

---

7   Eric Ripert Bio, Le-Bernardin Website, April 17, 2013, http://le-bernardin.com/about/#eric-ripert.

8   Frank Bruni, "Only the Four Stars Remain Constant," *New York Times*, March 16, 2005, http://events.nytimes.com/2005/03/16/dining/reviews/16rest.html?ref=ericripert.

year is something few companies or individuals can pull off, never mind someone whose business is as variable and subjective as cuisine.

At Manhattan's Art Director's Club, a modern temple for creative talent, I heard Ripert describe his approach to finding culinary inspiration. At his level, you might expect a signature style or a go-to dish, but Ripert refuses to rest on his laurels. If customers walk into his restaurant and ask for a specific entrée that they heard was his "specialty," he'll tell them it's out of stock and remove it from the menu before he ends up becoming known for a signature dish. While many chefs view a signature dish as an accomplishment, he believes it "means your success is in the past . . . [and] you're not inspiring to anyone. All the care you've put into the old dish dies because nobody cares anymore . . . You're not being creative anymore."[9]

Ripert's ruthless rejection of consistency has spawned more experimentation than many chefs might attempt in a lifetime. Constantly rotating his menu grants Ripert a deeper understanding of food pairings, taste combinations, and what it takes to adapt. By churning through hundreds of tastes, smells, and eclectic combinations, Ripert is blazing a culinary trail in a way similar to how Amancio Ortega pioneered fast fashion.

And it worked. If you want to experience his $332 Chef's Tasting Menu, reserve in advance, because despite astronomical pricing, his restaurant remains sold out weeks in advance.

Intentionally destroying your business model, products, and services can feel uncomfortable and even painful, but destruction enables unrestricted creativity while providing newfound flexibility and depth. Leading innovators often start from scratch—even make

---

9   Saabiri Chaudhuri, "Where the Passion Comes: One of America's Greatest Chefs Shares His Sources of Inspiration," *Fast Company*, March 28, 2008, http://www. fastcompany.com/772725/where-passion-comes-one-americas-greatest-chefs-shares -his-sources-inspiration.

a practice of regularly destroying prototypes or the latest iteration to spark urgency and unbridled thought. Individuals need to push themselves to learn new skills beyond those that seem tried and true. Companies must seek out opportunities to adapt and question the status quo constantly.

NERF GUNS, COLOR CRAYONS, AND CATAPULT WEAPONRY

It's one thing for an innovator such as Eric Ripert—who enjoys free rein over his menu and his kitchen without interference from anyone—to demonstrate the value of destroying one's creation intentionally, but it's quite another for an established company. That's a huge step—one that I thought long and hard about as I made the long drive out to Crayola's 6,000-employee Pennsylvania headquarters in the town of Easton.

The Crayola factory has fueled the local economy since 1903, when each individual crayon was carefully hand-wrapped by farmers' wives. As I neared Crayola, I couldn't help thinking about the dramatic impact of the digital age on arts and crafts. Will ubiquitous touch-screen tablets and interactive video games overwhelm the iconic maker of crayons and markers? What role will tangible arts and crafts play in the future of creative education? Do parents still consider crayon coloring a requisite building block of youth? Or are these classic products losing their relevance?

There was also a subtle irony in the company's market challenge. Known as an inspirer of youthful creativity, Crayola would have to summon its own inventiveness to connect with youths and parents bewitched by the digital age.

Upon entering the historic facility, I was greeted by Susan, the company's longtime receptionist, with a cheerful "Welcome to the world of color!" True to her greeting, Crayola's waiting room is a vibrant wax rainbow of walls adorned with roughly one hundred impressive children's crayon creations. I couldn't help feeling excited that the company's managers had agreed to my one peculiar request.

I really, really, wanted to tour the factory. We just strolled a few hundred yards and . . . *voilà!* There it was! It's an incredible site, an artistic twist on the fictional *Charlie and the Chocolate Factory*. Vats of Blizzard Blue–, Electric Lime–, and Razzmatazz-colored wax feed into massive machines run by workers imbued with a sense of purpose: fueling creativity and self-expression.

My clients escorted me through the factory floor to the "Creative Playground," the company's learning boardroom. The aroma of the wax crayons, tinged with vanilla, took me back, and that's no secret. My feelings of nostalgia are shared by millions worldwide.

More recently, Crayola has tackled a new challenge: boys. As dads have fixated on new gadgets and electronic toys, playtime with their sons has become a barrage of high-tech toys—from video games to remote-control helicopters to souped-up Nerf guns. And every time a dad engages his son in a video game or Nerf combat, a few less crayons splash across the page.

So, if you work for Crayola, how do you compete with the digital playtime habits of fathers and sons? It's not easy. Sharon DiFelice, Crayola's Innovation & Consumer Insights leader, told me, "It's hard to change what you feel so safe with." Historically, for Crayola, that safe space meant a marketplace defined as "arts, crafts, and stationery." That definition worked for a century, but when video games and laser tag started encroaching, Crayola realized it had become more important to focus on the customer experience. This observation spurred them to discard that outdated conception and replace it with a broader definition of the company's market—something it now refers to as "Children's Free Time."

To better understand that market, Crayola began to observe exactly what went on during that playtime. They noticed that little boys, unlike little girls, hunger for one repetitive pattern—

destruction. Once boys build the perfect block tower or line up all of their cars neatly, they topple those same towers and crash those cars, turning order into chaos. While young girls might proudly protect and even display their Crayola art, a little boy is a lot more likely to scribble it away.

Much like our intentionally destructive chef Eric Ripert, boys are predisposed to destroy. This key observation inspired Crayola to develop Create 2 Destroy, a clay work-kit that enables fathers and sons to construct their own castles. Once the edifices are complete, builders employ a catapult kit to facilitate the mutual destruction of each other's work. True to its name, the kit enables fathers and sons to create for the very purpose of destruction—just as Crayola itself did by destroying its outdated assumptions about where to plant its seeds and starting to hunt "prey" in new and unfamiliar ground.

Creative destruction is natural. It's not something to be feared or avoided. It's a force to accept and acknowledge, and best of all, you're already good at it. So channel your inner destructive child. Stop worrying so much about your current status quo and more about where the future can take you.

HIDDEN SECRETS, STARTING FRESH, AND A BILLIONAIRE AUTHOR

Legend has it that thousands of years ago, the phoenix soared as the king of birds, a mythical creature celebrated for its grandeur and immortality. But when it aged or was challenged by a foe, it would destroy itself. It would literally set itself on fire to be reborn from its own ashes. The point is that there comes a time when you need to imitate the phoenix. Destruction leads to creativity. The Black Plague, the London fires, Hurricane Katrina—all eventually spawned progressive change, from the Renaissance to modern London to major environmental initiatives to save our planet.

If the legend of the phoenix was skipped at your high school, it may ring familiar from J. K. Rowling's fifth blockbuster book, *Harry Potter and the Order of the Phoenix*. The metaphor of the phoenix is inspiring to an innovator, but it also captures the arc of J. K. Rowling's remarkable life. Rowling's first rags-to-riches story is a wonderful saga, but there's a second post–Harry Potter surprise few anticipated.

Born in the small English town of Yate, Rowling endured a childhood nearly as dark as the one she would one day imagine for Harry Potter. Her mother suffered from multiple sclerosis, and Rowling regarded her father as harsh and unsupportive. Despite Rowling's own difficult upbringing, she tried to brighten the life of her sister, Dianne. At six, Rowling began writing her first short stories, which she'd read aloud to inspire her four-year-old sister.

Rowling became an A student, achieving Head Girl, top of her class. She was accustomed to achieving her scholastic goals, so she was shocked when Oxford rejected her university application, spurning the woman who would become the world's first billionaire author. Left scrambling, Rowling ended up in Paris, studying French and the classics. That led to a low-paying stint as a bilingual secretary. Her life was off track. She was living in poverty. Then her mother died.

Rowling converted all that negativity into the energy to write her first book. She then moved to Portugal, where she married, gave birth, got divorced, and was forced to return home with nothing but three chapters of a children's book. With her life on the rocks, she felt like a failure, but years later, she would describe how failure and destruction can be liberating:

Failure meant a stripping away of the inessential. I stopped pretending to myself that I was anything other than what I was, and began to direct all my energy to finishing the only work that mattered to me. Had I really succeeded at anything else, I might never have found the determination to succeed in the one area where I truly belonged. I was set free, because my greatest fear had been realized, and I was still alive, and I still had a daughter whom I adored, and I had an old typewriter, and a big idea. And so rock bottom became a solid foundation on which I rebuilt my life.[10]

Like the phoenix, she emerged out of the ashes. Writing in cafés and barely scrimping by on state benefits, she finished the first book in the Harry Potter series on an old manual typewriter and then was devastated when the manuscript was rejected by a staggering twelve publishers. But she didn't give up hope. A year later, in 1996, Barry Cunningham of tiny Bloomsbury Publishing agreed to print her manuscript. He paid her a modest £1,500 advance, but warned her to get a day job. The rest is literary history. The Harry Potter series has become one of the most successful book franchises of all time, selling 450 million books and generating $15 billion. Rowling herself has earned an estimated $1 billion.

But if you're Rowling, what's next? As the world's most commercially successful author of children's books, the logical next act would be another children's series. The catch is that Rowling didn't want to write another children's series.

Her next effort, *The Casual Vacancy*, boldly ventured into adult mystery. Released in 2011, the novel was commercially successful but garnered mixed reviews. The *Guardian* said that it was "no masterpiece, but it's not bad at all,"[11] comparing it, as most reviews did, to the Harry Potter franchise: "It lacks the Harry Potter books' warmth and charm; all the characters are fairly horrible." Much of the book's criticism revolved around how it touched on topics not appropriate for Rowling's previous children's audience. As ignorant

---

10 "The Fringe Benefits of Failure," TED Talk by J. K. Rowling, 2008.

11 Theo Tait, "JK Rowling: The Casual Vacancy—Review," *Guardian* (London), September 26, 2012, http://www.theguardian.com/books/2012/sep/27/jk-rowling -casual-vacancy-review.

as they might seem, some of the Amazon one-star reviews included comments such as "My eight year old read this, I am disgusted by all the sex and drug use."

Rowling was feeling the sort of pressures that dominant companies often face when trying to follow up a hit product or banner year. Success sows a set of expectations, and the desire to please stakeholders can discourage hunting. But Rowling knew that as a creative writer, she couldn't pen another Harry Potter book without compromising her extraordinary series.

Like the phoenix, she needed to break free. For her next effort, Rowling abandoned the international clout of her personal brand and wrote under a pen name. Robert Galbraith, whose secrecy was vigilantly protected, was described by "his" publisher as "a former plainclothes Royal Military Police investigator who left in 2003 to work in the civilian security industry."[12]

Cuckoo's Calling was embraced by critics and crime writers, and three months later, the identity of the novel's real author leaked, and, predictably, sparked an avalanche of sales. But what Rowling most cherished was writing and publishing in a situation in which she was free to follow her own creative impulses. As she said during the media craze, "It has been wonderful to publish without hype or expectation and pure pleasure to get feedback under a different name."[13]

Remember: Whether you're an accomplished novelist, a successful CEO, or a would-be entrepreneur, past success creates barriers that both you and your customers must overcome. To innovate, you need to break free from past success.

---

12 Richard Brooks, "Whodunnit? J. K. Rowling's Secret Life as a Wizard Crime Writer Revealed," *Sunday Times* (London), July 14, 2013, http://www.thesunday times.co.uk/sto/news/uk_news/Arts/article1287513.ece.

13 Haroon Siddique, "JK Rowling Publishes Crime Novel Under False Name," *Guardian* (London), July 14, 2013, http://www.theguardian.com/books/2013/jul/14/jk-rowling-crime-novel-cuckoos-calling.

SUMMARY: THE HUNTER VS. THE FARMER

The traps that hold us back are often triggered by our own success. To avoid falling into them, we need to call on our hunter instincts.

TRAP 1: COMPLACENCY → BE INSATIABLE Complacency blocks curiosity. By experimenting, prototyping, and reassessing our assumptions, we can better understand when it's time to make a radical shift.

TRAP 2: REPETITION → STAY CURIOUS Repetition often prevents new ideas from being tested. When a booming enterprise starts to expand, there can be a strong tendency to template each store or office for consistency. Remember, this rigid repetition reduces the capacity for adaptation.

TRAP 3: PROTECTIVENESS → BE WILLING TO DESTROY At a certain point, to liberate potential it becomes necessary to destroy what has worked in the past.

Chapter 3

HOW TO RAISE A HUNTER

Raised in a shoe-box-sized house with just one main room, my father Sig learned early on to make the most out of what he was given. At age eight, he started his first business, selling unsold produce from a local grocery store. And over the next few years, the boy businessman expanded into door-to-door delivery of donuts, house supplies, and month-old magazines. By sixteen, he'd somehow managed to lease a nightclub venue, becoming the underage owner of a booze-less bar. I'm not sure what rules a teenager needs to bend to lease a nightclub, but my father made the deal happen.

One night, he rented his venue to a religious group. What he didn't realize was that the faithful also had a few unholy obsessions, including booze, gambling, and strippers. The police raided the joint and came looking for the person in charge, who happened to be at home working on his tenth-grade homework. His parents were understandably upset, but they would become even more furious when the next day's newspapers profiled the sixteen-year-old nightclub owner.

But to his peers, Sig was awesome.

Over the next fifty years, my father would repeat this pattern of finding value in neglected business opportunities. It didn't hurt that he exuded a charisma that forged friendships with all sorts of people. One day, he'd be trading stock tips with an oil tycoon, and the next, he'd be laughing with a construction worker he'd met down the street. When I was eighteen, he purchased a defunct lounge called the Roxbury. The previous owners spent over half a million dollars renovating the building into an upscale pool hall with a charming brick interior and an upside-down pool table mounted above the bar. Unfortunately, the upscale food and drink prices scared off customers, and my father plucked the lounge out of bankruptcy—for $175,000, roughly the price of the building.

He knew it took more than just good food and snappy décor to make a venue sparkle. Any entrepreneur needs to hustle to make things happen. He taught me that many people don't know how to follow through. While they may be passionate about their initial idea, they don't push hard enough.

Not Sig. He knocked on every door within a three-block radius. He wanted to meet every local, invite them for a drink, and let them know that the sleepy Roxbury was going to be the new hot spot. And soon enough it was. With customers now feeling as though they had a personal connection and invitation, the lounge turned around instantly.

Sig wasn't merely a hard worker. He drove himself to uncover opportunities that others might overlook—such as the time he realized that the hidden value of the Roxbury resided in the building's two-story outer wall. Where others saw merely a wall, he saw it as a blank canvas: one that faced one of the most popular downtown streets, and thus doubled as an advertising billboard that could generate $200,000 a year—more than what my father paid for the business.

Sig found opportunity in chaos. He was a true hunter.

CHOICE, CHALLENGE, AND THE UNDERDOG

One day, my father was presented with an extraordinary choice. He had extended a modest loan to the Calgary Stampeders, a Canadian Football League team that was struggling financially. Then the owner was caught up in a stock controversy and the team ended up in receivership. This strange twist had two consequences: My dad would never get his capital back, and his small loan made him the de facto owner. That is, *if* he chose to accept the enormous financial responsibility. While owning a sports team may sound glamorous, sports teams rank among the worst-performing investments, and my father had nowhere near deep enough pockets to survive a big loss.

The media forecast the team's demise just as my father pondered whether to take on this potentially costly burden. Without a savior, the Stampeders might fold or be forced to move to another city. Few knew that my dad was the debt holder and that the league was begging him to save the team. My mother, a social worker, had serious reservations. But to my father, an entrepreneur who'd grown up in a poor and rough-and-tumble neighborhood, owning a football team would signal that he'd made it. After all, how many people—even well-heeled people—own sports franchises? There was another factor. He was always tempted by the chance to execute a turnaround. His challenge was monumental: With an average attendance of just 13,000 per game, the franchise was an open wound, bleeding two million dollars per year. My dad couldn't cover further losses, but he felt the team had been mismanaged. He saw the potential to right these mistakes, so he accepted the liability of ownership. His friends, on the other hand, worried that he was in over his head.

Remembering the Roxbury, he formed three conclusions. The first was that the stadium possessed many untapped advertising opportunities, much like the Roxbury's outer wall. The second was that the stadium could be used to throw concerts, a new source of revenue. Third, and most important, he understood that attending a football game was an inherently social event and had a lot in common with going to a bar or restaurant. In other words, there would be a positive snowball effect if he could fill more seats and make the stadium feel like a party.

To raise attendance, he gave away thousands of tickets to the local children's hospital. And he promoted tailgate parties and entertainment that would turn each game into a festival. Traditional game announcers were replaced with colorful radio personalities. Dull halftime programs were replaced with massive, fan-focused games. For example, 200 fans would get to visit the sidelines where, on cue, they'd fire a mini-football toward the open windows of a moving car. Each football was marked with the fan's name, and if the fan landed a ball in the car, he or she would get a free ticket to the final season game. Repeat the ball-through-the-window feat at the final game, and you'd win the car. Over the course of ten games, 2,000 people got to visit the field—a huge proportion of the previous year's attendance.

He also went to great lengths to give "customers" his signature personal touch. If a fan had canceled his or her season tickets recently, they might get a call from my father or a player—for example, all-star quarterback Doug Flutie. If my dad called, he wasn't going to hang up until you were all-in. Then, during the games, he'd spend about five or ten minutes in one seat, and then move on to the next, meeting masses of hard-core fans. In his words, "I sat in nearly every damn seat of that stadium, and I made a lot of friends." He'd connect with people, thank them for being part of something, and ask them to bring their friends to the next game. He repeated this for dozens of games, meeting thousands of fans.

When asked about his team's prospects, my dad joked with the press, saying things like "We're the poorest team in the league . . . [We] can't afford to lose." There's nothing like being a popular underdog, and it seemed as though the whole city was rooting for the Stampeders. But my father's public joking also created a sense of urgency. If you wanted the team to stay in Calgary, now was the time to show your support.

Season-ticket holders were treated like insiders—each was sent a thank-you letter with a bumper sticker featuring the Stampeders' striking logo, a galloping white horse. The stickers went viral. It seemed that all 10,000 season-ticket holders adorned their vehicles with the white horse as a badge of honor. Within a few months, attendance doubled and the momentum was translating to a winning season on the field. The turnaround had begun.

A season later, the buzz turned into a roar, and the stadium was selling out with over 35,000 fans. The Stampeders had become the hottest event in town. It was the perfect business for my father. His down-to-earth, blue-collar roots and sense of humor matched those of the best sports fans. He was undoubtedly the only team owner ever to ride a horse, the team's mascot, into a hotel lobby (he was leading a team parade). That carefree nature and love of his city made him leaps and bounds more relatable than the average suit-wearing team owner. The few times he walked onto the field, the fans would start chanting, "Sig, Sig, Sig!"

Yet six years into his franchise-owning experiment, my father realized that he desperately needed a buyer. The team was finally profitable, but the debt burden was still insupportable.

In his more than half a decade of ownership, the Stampeders ranked first almost every year, playing in the semifinals five out of six times and winning the championship Grey Cup twice. In his final year, my dad was awarded permanent possession of the Keith Spaith Memorial Award, a distinction reserved for the most valuable player. He never played football, of course. But the award is given based on fan votes, and thousands had scratched the player names off the ballots, writing in Sig's name. I became the hunter I am today thanks to the lessons I learned from my father. Sadly, my father passed away shortly after I interviewed him, so I tell this story in his tribute.

SON OF SIG

A cowboy at heart, I grew up in rural Alberta, with one of those numberless rural addresses that require directions such as, "Keep goin' a few miles down the gravel road, till you get to the corner with the tractor parked next to the water well . . ." My childhood was spent riding dirt bikes, shooting my slingshot, and building stuff with my dad. Determined to invent something, anything, I was constantly scouring, prototyping, and searching for promising business ideas.

Although I grew up literally next to farmer fields, I realize now that my father's life lessons taught me to embrace the three hunter instincts:

INSATIABLE To stay inspired, we'd perpetually hunt for ideas together, devouring hundreds of magazines and newspapers. Our living room table was a collage of media. We'd flip through copies of *Popular Mechanics, Popular Science, Time, Newsweek, Car & Driver, Automobile, Motor Trend, The Economist, Fast Company, Inc., Forbes,* and *National Geographic.* We'd examine each new product, quizzing each other on whether it would be successful and how we might change it.

CURIOSITY While other boys were collecting shoe boxes of hockey cards, I'd clip out photos of the latest gizmos and gadgets I found most interesting (along with favorite advertisements) and stuff them into a few drawers. Sporting nerdy glasses, I walked around with a little red book for logging business ideas, such as a magnetic car, a humidifier/house fan, and a microwave that could mix and bake your cookies (who wouldn't want that). In some ways, that little red book was a precursor to the red-branded Trend Hunter website I'd launch twenty years later.

WILLING TO DESTROY Nearly every Saturday, my father and I would visit garage sales, liquidations, and wholesale stores, trying to figure out what new contraption we could fix or build. Using the scrap parts we bought that day, we'd build homemade remote-control cars, a vegetable steamer, and even a rocket-powered skateboard. Some of our creations were marvels, while others burst into flames. But I learned to prototype. And when we were finished, we'd move on to something new, which taught me to not become too protective of any one idea.

I learned to see entrepreneurship as an extension of these weekend projects. A friend once described my upbringing as the "Hogwarts School for Entrepreneurship," and years later, I can see the clear connection between how I was raised and my unusual path.

THE BEGINNING OF MY HUNT

My father inspired my hunger for entrepreneurship, but I didn't know what sort of business I wanted to start. In my second year at university, I tested my entrepreneurial genes, starting a twelve-person painting company. Armed with the recklessness of youth and an insatiable thirst for business, I assembled a team of friends and started marketing my College Pro Painting franchise. I worked an insane 130 hours a week, knocking on doors, signing up customers, training painters, and delivering paint. I loved it.

That summer, I tripled my district's numbers, setting College Pro's rookie record with $135,000 in revenue and $55,000 in profit. I'd proven to myself that I could be an entrepreneur. The catch was that I didn't want to run a painting business forever. My inner nerd needed a venture that encompassed two words: *dot* and *com*.

To accelerate my search, I majored in finance to study why some companies succeed and others fail. I spent thirty hours a week in an extracurricular program called Calgary Portfolio Management Trust (CPMT), helping to manage a portfolio for the University of Calgary's endowment fund. But I'd yet to find a business idea that was right for me. Betting on rising dot-com stocks seemed like the next-best option. I invested my entire $55,000 in painting profits into promising dot-coms. In a year, my $55,000 more than tripled to almost $200,000.

Then, just like M.C. Hammer, I became complacent about my success. Like so many others during that heady time, I misguidedly thought I was an investor with a magic touch. I moved on to the esoteric stuff—options, betting on the market's daily swings. In finance, it's the fastest way to triple your bet—or to go broke. My confidence was fed by computer programs I'd built to scan for trends and trading opportunities. I felt like a professional casino gambler capable of counting cards. But then, in April of 2000, the finance gods taught me a lesson. The Nasdaq crashed and my $200,000 collapsed to $50,000 in four stomach-churning days.

A longer-term effect was that my abrupt financial loss made me overly cautious. I was still hunting for a great business idea, but now I felt that it needed to be perfect. Instead of taking a risk, I'd spend the next decade pursuing a corporate path. In completing my Chartered Financial Analyst designation, I'd learn that what I was experiencing is called the snakebite effect. Once bitten by a big loss, people tend to become irrationally conservative. This trap ensnares gamblers, investors, and innovators alike, and it's similar to the farmer's trap of being too protective.

AN ALL-CONSUMING SEARCH

Eventually, I became a management consultant at The Monitor Group to learn about different industries and to gain experience helping Fortune 500 CEOs evaluate their new ventures. After that, I earned my MBA and Chartered Financial Analyst designation, all the while searching for an appropriate entrepreneurial idea. Wanting to get my hands dirty on real-world projects, I started working at Capital One.

My corporate career was tracking well, but I knew that I was disappointing my inner entrepreneurial self. I'd burned through a decade of peak working years helping other companies and brands while shortchanging my own entrepreneurial dreams. I was desperate for a business idea.

It was then that I started Trend Hunter. I thought that if I built a place where people from around the world could share business ideas, someone, somewhere, would surely contribute an idea that could inspire my next venture. What I didn't realize was that Trend Hunter *itself* would become my big idea.

By day, I continued to log fifty hours a week at Capital One, but I was pouring even more hours into Trend Hunter in the evenings and on weekends. As the site grew, I kept upping my mental—and dollar—investment. I actually made my first hire while I was still working full time. Bianca Bartz, an ambitious young contributor, became our first editor, editing the daily issue from her makeshift Starbucks office a few thousand miles away.

Over the next year, Trend Hunter caught fire. Seemingly overnight, we'd become an international army of hunters, tracking down thousands of new ideas for millions of like-minded people. Ironically, MTV described me as being "on the forefront of cool,"[1] unaware that by day I was a director at a bank. Yet, my Capital One banking background conferred a positive benefit. It led me to think of the website not as a media publication but as a giant consumer research lab, an early experiment in big data and crowdsourcing.

---

1   "Trend Spotting," *MTV News,* June 22, 2006.

On my thirtieth birthday, I made the entrepreneurial leap to hunt trends full time. Unlike most start-ups, we already had momentum and an advertising revenue stream, so we never had to take on venture capital. Two billion views and several hundred clients later, we've developed a proven, battle-tested method for identifying patterns and finding better ideas faster—the very method I'm going to share with you for the remainder of this book.

By now, you have a good sense of the traps to be avoided and how to awaken your hunter instincts. Next up is the fun part, the easy part—those patterns that will change the way you see the world and enable you to spot opportunity wherever you turn.

Part II

Hunt

Chapter 4

GETTING MOMENTUM ON YOUR SIDE

I f you want to find that hot new idea that could revolutionize your career or business and maybe even change your life, awakening your inner hunter is a good start. But how can you find better opportunities faster? How can you regularly outsmart, out-adapt, and out-maneuver competitors? To win, you need to know where to hunt and how to leverage the momentum of your environment.

Several hundred years ago, millions of wild buffalo roamed North America. Just one of these 2,000-pound beasts could feed your family for months and provide leather and fur for clothing and shelter. But attempting to take down a buffalo is extraordinarily dangerous. The beasts are big, surprisingly fast, and well aware of how to protect themselves. If you tried to sneak into a pack to kill just one, you'd likely be trampled. But what if you could channel the herd to your advantage?

Near the border between northern Montana and southern Alberta lies an ancient Blackfoot hunting ground called Head-Smashed-In Buffalo Jump. The rather foreboding name refers to a steep cliff that was used to kill herds of buffalo. Instead of hunting smaller game, or attempting to pick off one buffalo at a time, the Blackfoot braves developed a clever strategy. They'd simply wait until a herd appeared in the nearby Porcupine Hills. Then "buffalo runners" would dress up as coyotes and wolves to scare the giant beasts until they were all stampeding in one direction. As the buffalo raced to escape, they'd get trapped by their own momentum—at which point the waiting braves would divert them down a specific path that led right off the cliff. Each hunt would reap dozens of buffalo, providing abundant food and fur for the tribe to survive the winter.

The lesson is that in trying to master big forces—whether they be buffalo herds, megatrends, or large competitors—momentum can give you an edge. You need to coordinate your attack, and then use the features and patterns of your environment to your advantage. This chapter will show you how.

THE SIX PATTERNS OF OPPORTUNITY

Just as Robert Lang developed a mathematics for the patterns of origami, Trend Hunter is developing a mathematics for the patterns of innovation. To date, we've studied a quarter-million ideas. By examining the choices and behaviors of the 100 million people who have visited our site, we've gained critical intelligence about the newest, fastest-evolving trends and ideas. Using our website as a high-tech innovation laboratory, we've studied 10 million hours of behavior and tracked several billion consumer choices. This kind of data-intensive research into innovation has never before been possible, and the results are fascinating. One of the most powerful concepts to emerge from this work is that, across all industries, opportunity seems to follow six major patterns: convergence, divergence, cyclicality, redirection, reduction, and acceleration (all of which will be explained shortly).

Traditionally, trend-spotters have tried to categorize the world based on megatrends, such as environmentalism, the rise of China, or social media, to name a few. However, this approach is limited, because megatrends are obvious and your competitors already know them. Quite simply, recognizing them doesn't provide a unique competitive advantage. What we've uncovered, and market-tested with our Fortune 1000 clients, is that it's much more valuable to identify the patterns of opportunity that a megatrend or big business might, in the future, create. Turns out, it's not about *what's* happening; it's about searching for what could happen *next*.

Specifically, there are six major patterns of opportunity that are created by nearly every major breakthrough product. Thus, you can use these patterns to predict or uncover future business opportunities that will be indirectly fueled by a burgeoning megatrend associated with that product. Much like the way the Blackfoot tribe would redirect the flow of a stampeding herd of buffalo, you can redirect the momentum of another company's success to your advantage. It may seem counterintuitive, but this phenomenon is something we've spotted time and time again at Trend Hunter. Competition can become an asset if you know how to channel it. By the time you're done reading the chapters that follow, you may be genuinely wishing your competitors all the success in the world.

Here is what I mean. Imagine if you'd been inspired by the early growth of Facebook, already a thriving success by 2006. Had you tried to compete with Facebook head-on, it would have been like trying to hold back a herd of stampeding buffalo. But Facebook created patterns of opportunity. The trick to spotting them was to deconstruct the social network's main functions. Functionally, Facebook was (1) a network for just your friends, (2) a permanent archive of your photos, and (3) a place to share your everyday life.

To uncover opportunity, you would analyze these three aspects of Facebook through the lens of different patterns. An easy example would be *divergence*—finding the opposite of the mainstream. Because Facebook focused on networking friends, there might emerge, for instance, a need for a network that wasn't just for friends. Enter Twitter, a place where a person can "follow" random strangers. Meanwhile, the permanence of Facebook as a personal archive breeds fear that photos might be seen by those who shouldn't see them, inhibiting the ability to share freely. This could well spawn a craving for something temporary. Enter SnapChat, a place for sharing temporary photos, which showed up to the party half a decade late, but still grew big enough to turn down a $4 billion offer from Google. Finally, although Facebook's mechanism for sharing people's everyday lives can be useful and empowering, it also leads to oversharing and an Internet flooded with amateur smartphone photos. If you happen to be a lover of photographic art, you might want to bring the art back. Enter Instagram, a billion-dollar business that adds artistic filters to your mobile photos.

The point is that none of the companies—not even Google—has been successful at directly taking on Facebook. The quicker, smarter, easier path to success is to hunt for the patterns of opportunity that a company, trend, or breakthrough might create.

Once you learn all six patterns of opportunity, you'll be more adept at spotting how winning business ideas get created, making you a better innovator, decision maker, and investor.

CONVERGENCE   DIVERGENCE   CYCLICALITY   REDIRECTION   REDUCTION   ACCELERATION

Chapter 5

CONVERGENCE

CONVERGENCE: Creating a winning business or product by combining multiple products, services, or trends. Includes: mixing, product integration, social integration, bringing people together, adding value through layering, drama, multifunctions, and co-branding.

Though you might not realize it, you experience convergence daily. You stop at Starbucks for some fair-trade coffee, self-indulgence, Internet access, and a familiar haunt that feels like your "third place" between home and the office. When you arrive home, you take a leisurely stroll around town, humming to the beat of music streamed on your smartphone and guided by the phone's GPS maps. All the while, you keep in touch with your friends by tweeting or sending photos from that very same phone. Half an hour later, you meet some friends for a quick bite. Depending on which tapas joint, wine bar, or restaurant you've picked out, you're soon enjoying California cuisine, Asian fusion, veggie burritos, sushi pizza, or some other culinary collage that is a convergence of flavor and culture.

Tap into convergence just right and it can be explosive. Convergence can spawn entire industries. Snowboarding's meteoric growth was all about thunderous convergence patterns—a heart-thumping mash-up of skateboarding, surfing, skiing, music, fashion, and youth's natural need to rebel. The elements blended so potently that the newly invented sport quickly became a popular lifestyle that far outstripped the individual sports that helped inspire it.

We see obvious examples of convergence in tech devices, such as our mobile phones that also act as computers, cameras, music players, and gaming consoles, but convergence can also be powerful in traditional industries. Think of gas stations merged with convenience stores, grocery store/sandwich shops, pharmacy/post offices, department store/fast-food outlets, bookstore/cafés, and restaurant/ Wi-Fi hot spots.

At first, convergence seems like an easy pattern to grasp, but plenty of companies have rushed into convergence without sufficiently understanding the concept. For example, Nokia knew people liked both video games and mobile phones, so the company eagerly launched the N-Gage video game phone. Unfortunately, rather than embrace the benefits of a two-in-one device, consumers saw a clunky phone combined with a lackluster gaming device. The N-Gage looked like a badly designed TV remote with a tiny screen. It was a colossal failure.

It's simply not enough to combine two ideas. Colgate, for instance, sought to tie people's need for hygiene with the rise in healthy eating. The company took a gamble and combined its hygiene brand with healthy eating, launching Colgate Kitchen Entrees, a line of ready-made meals. Consumers were perplexed. Toothpaste, mouthwash, and frozen foods don't have a lot in common other than that they all go in your mouth, and not surprisingly, the frozen meals tanked.

Yet when convergence is done smartly, it can be one of the most straightforward ways to take advantage of emerging trends. In this chapter, you'll meet convergence in its many powerful forms, from products to services to immersive experiences.

PRISON TATTOOS AND AN OXFORD EDUCATION

More than twenty years ago, an art history undergraduate named Kyla found herself visiting Germany's Neue Pinakothek galleries with her family. The young academic soon began sharing the secrets and scandal behind each painting. Within minutes, half a dozen tourists were eagerly tagging along, treating her as if she were the gallery's curator. When it came to art, Kyla was a cut above. Give her a few hours with an art history textbook, and she'd absorb every fact, figure, date, and dimension.

Her virtuoso abilities earned her a perfect undergraduate GPA and a scholarship to the prestigious University of Oxford, where she became one of the rare scholars to receive a complimentary *viva voce,* meaning that after one oral and written exam, she was awarded her master's degree and fast-tracked into the school's doctoral program.

Then came the curveball. She was diagnosed with ovarian cancer and given a fifty-fifty chance of survival.

Determined to achieve her academic goals, Kyla battled cancer while continuing her quest to be an extraordinary professor. Despite the effects of the chemo, she'd frequently pull all-nighters to perfect her lectures. The only thing that sank her spirits was something an outsider might dismiss as insignificant: her eyebrows. As she explained to me, "After chemotherapy treatments, you can put a wig on your head, but there's something totally different about losing your eyebrows. It's a reminder that you're not normal."

Kyla asked her oncology nurse what she could do about it. Kyla was encouraged when she learned that her hospital did have medically safe tattooing equipment, but she soon discovered there were some extreme drawbacks. The machines were crude and the staff's tattooing skills limited. Kyla's tattooed eyebrows turned out comically asymmetrical. Not wanting to make them worse, she searched for a traditional tattooist to repair the hospital's handiwork. But the tattooist she selected also blundered—by using an ink with metallic pigments. When Kyla got her next MRI, the machine's powerful magnets tore at the pigments, triggering an allergic reaction and bleeding.

Concerned, Kyla's oncologist urged her to pursue a less-stressful life, pointing out that her high-pressure academic career might threaten her chances for survival. But Kyla had another plan in mind.

KYLA'S AWAKENING

Forced to consider what really mattered, Kyla found herself taking on the role of a hunter. Was there a fresh realm where she could find passion and meaning? She didn't really recognize it at the time, but this was her awakening. Often, a difficult transition period is the point at which people tap into their hidden potential.

If Kyla couldn't carry on as a professor, what else might quench her thirst for achievement? She kept thinking about her eyebrow disaster. Could she invent a better way to make restorative tattoos? She knew nothing of tattooing or plastic surgery, but yearned to help others avoid what she'd had to go through.

Curious and highly motivated, she began her search for ideas in the strangest of places: prison.

CHAOS CREATES OPPORTUNITY

Adversity—whether due to an illness, economic pressures, or a lost job—can present tremendous opportunity. When our security is threatened, complacency isn't a realistic strategy. In that situation, you're far more willing to destroy what's worked in the past and more likely to become insatiable in your quest for something new.

Just as J. K. Rowling's dire poverty helped inspire her to take her extraordinarily creative path to Harry Potter, and just as Michelin-starred chef Eric Ripert abandons his best dishes to start from scratch, starting fresh can heighten our ability to spot key trends.

After many years of consulting work with several hundred CEOs and companies, I've identified three basic attitudes toward adversity and change: paranoia, confidence, and desperation. On the surface, it would seem as though a confident attitude is most beneficial. But in fact, the opposite is true. Perhaps not surprisingly, most companies place themselves in the confident category. They tend to celebrate past successes and focus on optimizing tried-and-true strategies. That sense of confidence suppresses the feeling of urgency, inhibiting adaptation. In contrast, desperate companies know that the status quo won't save them. Slipping sales or fast-declining market share can spark a fervor that boosts innovation. Apple, for instance, only brought back Steve Jobs when the company was on the verge of bankruptcy and was desperate to pursue reinvention. The company's fear of failure enabled Jobs to make bold bets that would eventually lead to Apple's epic success.

Similarly, there was a time when IBM's seemingly invincible computer business was floundering. The company was losing billions of dollars a year. Headed for collapse in the early 1990s, IBM brought in a new CEO, Louis Gerstner. With little to lose, Gerstner strategically shed computer lines, pushed people to reimagine their potential, and inspired a sense of urgency for change that helped IBM pivot and reinvent itself as a successful services firm.

Finally, consider the example of General Motors. For decades, the automaker dominated car sales in the United States. In the 1990s, it picked up on the rise of the SUV and America's love for trucks, skewing its lineup to include the lumbering Tahoe and the 8,600-pound Yukon. From 1990 to 2004, "mega-horsepower" was a good bet. The annual sales of light trucks went from a low 20 percent of the market to over half of all consumer vehicles sold in the

United States.[1] Sure, the company was struggling with a bloated cost structure, but trucks and solid demand helped GM fend off its foreign rivals.

However, in the five years that followed, fashions flipped. The trend in the proportion of trucks sold reversed. Millions of consumers switched to lighter, more-economical cars. Then the recession started, banging the last few nails into GM's coffin. With a market already in downturn, a bloated cost structure, and an out-of-step-with-the-zeitgeist product line, the company fell into bankruptcy. By 2009, the number of GM vehicles sold in the United States was down 56 percent.[2] For context, over the same period, Toyota's 2009 numbers were down just 14 percent.

GM used the crisis to reengineer its approach. It abandoned the Hummer and launched a fleet of lighter vehicles. As the market turned, sales grew, and so, too, did GM's lead over Toyota. Even when safety recalls threw the company into crisis in 2014, GM's strong product line continued to attract customers to its dealer showrooms.

Anyone can tap into urgency, and it doesn't require looking down the barrel of such dire circumstances. Indeed, some of the world's most profitable companies are driven by an almost maniacal zeal to scratch out new advances. Many exhibit the third basic attitude toward change—what I sometimes refer to as "good" paranoia. Organizations that practice it don't necessarily have to be motivated by adversity. Google, for example, is famous for its outrageous, blue-sky gambles, from driverless cars to Google +, to Google Glass. Many are crapshoots, but enough are breakthroughs that they more than make up for the flops. Driven by an almost maniacal fear of

---

1   Energy.gov Market Share of New Cars vs. Light Trucks, 1975–2008, http://energy.gov/eere/vehicles/fact-553-january-12-2009-market-share-new-cars-vs-light-trucks.

2   GM U.S. New Vehicle Sales vs. Toyota U.S. New Vehicle Sales, 2004, 2009, 2013 Company Reports, Wikipedia.

losing dominance, companies such as Google inculcate in their employees the mind-set that they must do everything possible to stay number one. These companies create a culture of urgency by cannibalizing their own products and by perpetually experimenting.

The lesson is that to fight success-bred complacency, you need to be insatiably curious, open to intentional destruction, and just a little bit paranoid.

KYLA'S NEW DIRECTION

Illness helped Kyla see the potential of a new direction. Compelled to abandon her beloved Oxford, she dove into tattooing as if she were researching a doctoral dissertation. Like any good idea-hunter, she began her quest by searching the world for clues and resources, soaking up every tidbit of existing information on tattoo history, culture, science, equipment, and techniques. As she entered uncharted territory, she quickly surmised that she'd need to solve three major problems. First, she'd have to find pigments that could be injected into a cancer patient's skin, which is normally too sensitive to handle foreign particles and dyes. Second, she'd require superior techniques and equipment capable of re-creating human features, such as eyebrows, skin pigment, or three-dimensional areola. Third, she'd need to find tattoo inks that mimic natural skin tones—no easy task.

Kyla met and studied under plastic surgeons, tattoo artists, and micro-pigmentation specialists in London, Vancouver, and Paris. She even apprenticed with a Japanese ink master revered by Yakuza gangsters (members of organized-crime groups in Japan), who are renowned for their elaborate use of tattoos to mark accomplishment, affiliation, and rank. The Yakuza gangsters and their battle scar–mimicking tattoos led Kyla to her next big breakthrough. She'd already tackled part of the challenge by discovering a special type of medical micro-pigmentation that used safe pigments. To solve the rest of her problems, she'd literally have to go behind bars.

CRIMINAL INSPIRATION

Visit a prison and you'll see dramatic evidence of the signaling power of tattoos: A teardrop tattoo underneath the eye announces you've murdered someone; stars on the knees mean you'll kneel for nobody; and a clock with no hands means you've been dealt a life sentence. And yet, ironically, all of this skin artwork is the product of wild improvisation. In the typical prison tattoo artist's toolbox, you'll find such quirky items as guitar strings, magnets, washers, and a Walkman motor. Unfortunately, these makeshift parts and materials often exact a heavy cost, as they dramatically increase the spread of blood-borne pathogen diseases such as hepatitis and AIDS.

No surprise, then, that prison tattoos are illegal.

Thus, getting a tattoo in prison is a covert affair. The problem is that piercing your skin with guitar wire hooked up to a Walkman engine will cause your flesh to swell, and swollen, welted skin signals that someone's getting inked, which can earn the offender a long stint in solitary confinement. That represents a quandary for a prisoner desperately seeking a tattoo, and as we've seen, tough problems can inspire creative ideas. With years to explore solutions, many prisoners have developed extremely clever techniques to minimize the skin irritation of a tattoo—techniques overlooked that could help Kyla better tattoo cancer patients with sensitive skin. She tracked down prison tattoo artists, shared her story, bonded with them over their mutual love of art, and learned their secret techniques for implanting pigment with minimal irritation. It's an unusual tale, but there's an important lesson here that many of us often miss: Clinging to conservative methods rather than challenging the status quo often means forfeiting the possibility of something brilliant and inspired.

COMBINING OLD AND NEW

Kyla had found one of her breakthroughs in prison, but she still faced another challenge: how to replicate the extraordinary colors of human skin. For that, she called on her knowledge of art history and reached back several hundred years to a genius who disrupted the world of art.

Sometimes, in creating a fresh idea, your best move is to draw on ideas from the past. For instance, Twitter's remarkably successful, simple home page design and proportions were inspired by the golden ratio, which dates back 2,400 years and was favored by classical architects and countless great artists.

As an art professor, Kyla knew the value of history. She also knew that during an amazing stretch of the sixteenth century, some of the greatest painters of all time—men such as Da Vinci, Raphael, Michelangelo, Tintoretto, Veronese, and Titian—were locked in bitter rivalries and intense competition. Among the questions they battled over was who could create the best skin tone on canvas.

Tiziano Vecelli, better known as Titian, was considered the master of his generation—even by Leonardo da Vinci. At twelve, Titian apprenticed to another painter, but critics immediately favored the youngster's work. Titian quickly became nationally renowned, leading to extreme popularity and a career of commissioned work. Like many great artists, Titian inspired copycats and jealous rivals, who even employed spies posing as students in a flagrant attempt to steal his secrets. They couldn't unravel one central mystery, however: How did Titian achieve such luminous skin tones? Other artists simulated skin by mixing pinks and browns, yet Titian's paintings glowed with multiple levels of color. Even da Vinci was forced to acknowledge that Titian was the first to capture the luminescence of skin.

Titian's secret technique required unconventional thought. Traditionally, painters would mix one color and add grays and whites to create shading. However, Titian had been inspired by the way Murano stained-glass artisans would create different coloring through layers of colored glass. Importing this technique to his own field, Titian thinned his paints with egg whites and linseed oil. Then he'd brush on multiple coats, each slightly different. By layering multiple glazes of color, he'd achieve astonishingly realistic-looking skin—no small skill in an age when nude paintings were the erotica of the day.

In a glorious "Eureka!" moment, Kyla thought of Titian. She quickly began developing and patenting a pigment dispersant product she named the Titian Wash, which would enable tattooists to use similar layering tactics in the dermal layer of the skin. Unlike traditional opaque tattoos, Kyla's layering yields more realistic, natural layers of color, simulating the translucency Titian achieved on canvas.

By combining advances in micro-pigmentation, prison tattooist skills, and Titian's centuries-old secret techniques, Kyla launched a unique new business named Cosmetic Transformations. Over the next five years, she performed several thousand procedures, camouflaging burns, erasing scars, restoring eyebrows, and re-creating areolas. She helped cancer patients, movie stars, military veterans, and victims of attack.

To those who witnessed Kyla's art history prowess on that long-ago tour of German art galleries, her success might seem natural, even expected. I was one of the lucky few tagging along that day. Kyla Gutsche happens to be my sister.

Though people rarely recognize it, adversity can breed innovation. My sister started by identifying a pain point and then mixed and matched potential solutions until she came up with something incredible. If something bugs you or triggers your curiosity, pay attention: there may be a creative combination of ideas that could turn into a big business idea. And remember that your personal passions and skills could be the rich source of creativity that gets you to that solution faster.

Most important, none of this requires an Oxford degree. Convergence comes easily when you're open to ideas and pushing yourself to look for patterns and combinations.

In the case of Kyla, convergence led to an entirely new product and service, but convergence can also power an existing product and service to new heights.

CRYSTAL METH, CONVICT LABOR, AND KILLER BREAD

Dave Dahl is a man of contradictions. Brawny yet soft-spoken, pumped up with the muscles of a bodybuilder, he resembles a 1980s heavy-metal rock star with his long, flowing hair and bushy moustache. It's unlikely you'd guess that he's in the rather traditional business of baking bread. But Dahl's father was a pioneer, founding the family's Portland, Oregon–based Midway Bakery, a small shop that was among the first to sell all-grain loaves made without animal fats.

As a young man, Dahl couldn't muster much love for the bread business. Though all the Dahl children were expected to work in the bakery, Dave lacked his father's passion and felt trapped. Ultimately, he rebelled and began a long descent into depression and drug addiction. Crystal-meth madness plunged him into a two-decade roller-coaster ride of drug deals, exotic dancers, armed robbery, and high-speed car chases that ended with a long stretch in prison.

In the slammer, Dahl sought medical help for depression. For the first time, he felt normal, and he was eager to repay those whom he'd harmed, including his own family. He imagined how his life would be different if he'd joined the family bakery. Dreaming of redemption, he began researching everything he could about the world of bread.

Upon his release, Dahl pleaded for a job with the family firm, now called NatureBake. His brother Glenn was reluctant to give his sibling another chance—and for good reason. Dave had robbed and trashed the family bakery more than once during his meth-crazed years. But Glenn recognized the shift in his brother's tone, and in 2004, Dave was brought back on the payroll. Determined to prove himself through hard work and dedication, he logged hundred-hour weeks. He filled in for absent workers, cleaned up the kitchen, and diligently experimented with new recipes. He was going to make a difference, starting with his first big idea: Dave's Killer Bread! Dahl never killed anyone, but he believed his fresh recipes were "killer good" and hoped the shocking label would intrigue customers.

In the summer of 2005, Dahl brought a hundred loaves of his Killer Bread to the Portland Farmers' Market. The loaves, packed with sunflower, pumpkin, flax, and sesame seeds, were an instant hit, selling out in hours. By the end of the summer, Dave's Killer Bread had been picked up by top grocery chains such as New Seasons, Co-Op, Whole Foods, and Fred Meyer. The national distribution deals were an opportunity to take NatureBake to the next level and expand Dahl's creative leadership. Soon, the brand had a fresh swagger and authenticity. The website was hand-drawn in a colorful, cartoonish style and featured captivating videos, a capsule version of "Dave's Story," and a sketch of a ripped Dave Dahl strumming a guitar and standing behind bars. The marketing and story worked not only because it was genuine and creative—the bread also happened to be terrific. "It would be easy to think this is a crunchy gimmick—ex-con does good with organic flour, insuring the triumph of the crunchy Northwest," wrote the *New York Times*.

"But Dave's Killer Bread is actually the best bread I've ever bought in a supermarket."[3]

Dahl's initial success—the Dave's Killer Bread name and attitude—sprang from a concept Trend Hunter calls "shock labeling," which is part of the divergence pattern you'll learn more about in the next chapter. For examples of shock labels, think about catchy wine labels such as Jesus Juice, Fat Bastard, and Dirty Laundry, or, in a different aisle of the supermarket, the caffeine-happy Cocaine Energy Drink. But while divergence propelled the bakery's initial growth, it was convergence—and specifically, Dahl's mixing of a number of trends—that caused the company to soar.

THE SHOTGUN APPROACH

Marketing Dahl's prison past was good business, fitting squarely within the popular trend of bad-boy imagery. Even better, Dahl's story was one of redemption. His journey, philosophy, and imagery appeared throughout the bakery's marketing materials and website. The brand echoed other shock-label brands and also leveraged pop culture's fixation with prisons, which in recent years has led to prisoner-designed couture, prison-styled homes, and correctional facilities converted into hotels.

The company describes how Dahl aspired to "make the world a better place, one loaf of bread at a time."[4] He trained fellow former inmates to bake, and he launched an aggressive donation plan, which now amounts to an annual gift of 325,000 loaves to Meals on Wheels People, Helping Hands, and Sisters of the Road. Dahl

---

3   Alex Kuczynski, "Obsessions: Dave's Killer Bread," *New York Times*, January 20, 2010.

4   Dave's Killer Bread company website, http://www.daveskillerbread.com/faq .html, retrieved September 2, 2014.

was tapping into an embedded social good trend that was rippling throughout the Pacific Northwest and had gained a foothold with such leading Seattle brands as the Body Shop and Starbucks.

So many social business models emerged in the new millennium that in 2011, Trend Hunter co-launched a channel, SocialBusiness .org, dedicated to combining or converging a social cause within for-profit businesses. TOMS Shoes is a rich example of a "one-for-one" social entrepreneurship model that has been widely imitated. Every time a consumer buys a pair of TOMS shoes, the company gives a pair to a child in Africa or some other developing continent. These embedded social models not only make the planet a better place, they foster respect for the brand.

Dahl also leapt on "organic local," the trend of serving organic and locally sourced food. His rejection of preservatives and genetically modified ingredients inspired the double-entendre slogan, "Just say no to bread on drugs," which adorns the packaging of each loaf of bread. The grains are also locally sourced, supporting local farmers while reducing the need for long-haul transportation. Dahl even launched a bicycle delivery service to develop a carbon-free method to distribute Dave's Killer Bread to local shops.

Two other trends Dahl capitalized on are "eco manufacturing" and "living wages." The bakery's new plant is fueled by wind power, eliminating 1,100,000 pounds of CO_2 emissions each year, and employees are paid based on a standard of "living wages" (similar to the "fair wage" that Starbucks championed).

By smartly combining so many individual trends, Dahl's family business vastly increased its chances of success. Indeed, convergence helped propel this small company from a modest single bakery into a $50 million enterprise with 240 employees, seventeen varieties of organic bread, and a new retail location, appropriately called Mother Truckers. The company's profits continue unabated, and the family sold a major stake to a New York equity firm in late 2012.

Those looking to reap the profit from their own fifty-million-dollar business should take note that Dahl began with relentless experimentation. His pent-up need to make a difference provoked meticulous recipe testing that created a product worth a premium. And his countless experiments extended far beyond the kitchen, including innovation in production, recruiting, marketing, and community involvement. His biggest breakthrough came from realizing that he could turn weakness into advantage. By drawing attention to his troubled past, he tapped into the widespread sympathy many have for the underdog.

Once you craft a strong core idea, you can often increase your likelihood of success by riding multiple trends. Dave's Killer Bread succeeds because the abundance of hot trends it exploits makes the firm's products easier for consumers to love. All too often, a company or entrepreneur launches a new concept or brand that is incomplete. It needs something more to separate it from the pack. Convergence is part of the continuous hunt for trends or ideas that can help propel your business to further success.

GPS, ZOMBIES, AND THE POWER OF STORY

A decade into the cold war, the Soviets and Americans fiercely competed at everything from chess to Olympic medal counts to nuclear warheads to the race to be the first in space. In 1957, the Soviets leaped ahead with the launch of *Sputnik,* a man-made satellite, into space. America's attention was now focused on the purpose of the mysterious satellite—and how to monitor its transmissions. This mission led two American scientists, William Guier and George Weiffenbach, to a breakthrough that would forever change how you find your way to your holiday resort or navigate a new city. They discovered what would later become the Global Positioning System, or GPS.

Their basic discovery was that by using physics principles from the early 1800s, they could pinpoint *Sputnik*'s exact location from the ground. Used in reverse, the same discovery led Americans to realize that if they positioned several satellites in the sky, they could track objects on earth. It was pattern recognition at its best. Although it would take decades to complete, America's GPS satellite network was fully functional for military use by 1995. A year later, it was clear that GPS could have so many applications that President Bill Clinton opened up the technology for civilian use.

Early applications were simple but game-changing, including maps, emergency rescue, fleet tracking, and navigation. Next, innovators found ways to incorporate GPS into global scavenger hunts, tourism, and even athletic training. For example, in 2006, AllSport released a phone app for runners and bikers to track their routes, elevation changes, and average speeds. I myself used AllSport on my vintage BlackBerry to track my top speed in downhill skiing.

Meanwhile, Nike had been adding the technology to wearable devices, launching the Nike Sportsband and Nike+iPod for the gym. Nike's convergence of GPS navigation and athletic wear made it possible for people to track their cardio and workouts. In 2010, the company took another step when it released Nike+Running, which allowed people to not only track their run, but also share daily accomplishments with their social networks.

As social media exploded into the mainstream, Foursquare brought GPS to personal networking, quickly gaining 20 million users in its first three years. By 2012, people everywhere were using Foursquare to declare virtual "mayorship" of their favorite coffee shops, tourist locations, and hipster bars—a digital badge of honor for being the most frequent visitor to a location.

As the television show *The Walking Dead* brought zombies into pop culture, a new twist on GPS was born. Zombies, Run! is a multidimensional running experience that combines your favorite music, GPS tracking, and the narrative of a heart-pounding zombie horror story. Pick your jogging path, and start running to the pace of a zombie drama that overrides the music. The iPhone app's marketing description reads, "Get Fit. Escape Zombies. Become a Hero." If your pace slows down, you'll be warned that the zombies are catching up. Head toward a building, and you'll be told to sprint to grab supplies. Immersed in an interactive story that's constantly tracking your location, you'll likely run faster.

On the surface, the convergence of these two trends—zombies and running—seems highly unlikely. But that's exactly why it worked. Astonishingly, the zombie app was funded in 2012 through a meager $73,000 crowd-funding campaign. Within two years, nearly a million runners were fleeing zombies everywhere.

From space satellites to zombies, the brief history of GPS serves as a classic example of how ideas can be reinvented and reimagined by combining them in imaginative ways.

FIGHT CLUB, BATTLING UNEMPLOYMENT, AND SECRET LOCATIONS

The turbulent global economy has heaped more pressure on countless young people to find work. In North America and Europe, millennial underemployment has become so chronic that parents everywhere are finding their twenty-five-year-old children living at home and pursuing what often seems like perpetual education. But how do you find your calling if you're an underemployed graduate? Can you blend your passion and education into a new venture?

Ned Loach and Robert Gontier were two highly educated millennials looking for work and a greater purpose in life. Each had earned multiple degrees and certifications in the arts, but the extra qualifications left them wanting more. So the two dreamed of a way to channel their passions and create something incredible.

Imagine you're preparing to leave work Friday afternoon when you receive the week's most anticipated e-mail, a cryptic note that reveals a secret location and bare-bones instructions: "Be at the old distillery at 4:00 p.m. tomorrow. Wear black."

What's up? The following afternoon, you nervously venture to the dilapidated distillery. The area seems deserted, but wait a minute . . . what's that? There's an abandoned car, concrete walls, dim lighting, and a taped-off crime scene. You press ahead into a surging crowd, joining several hundred similarly outfitted attendees who are all wearing the same look of intrigue. Could this be a scene from a movie? But what movie? As you step deeper into the factory setting, a fight breaks out. Seemingly sober corporate-types are squaring off in a makeshift fight ring. But this is no boxing ring. It's a bare, factory-like industrial space with concrete walls. The dimly hostile space is oddly intriguing.

After being teased with a few more clues, you piece it together— you've been transported to *Fight Club*! A waitress seemingly right out of the film offers you a drink while asking if you'd like your nose broken or face bruised (makeup artists are on hand). Soon, you're summoned to another concrete room and the theatrical experience turns cinematic. *Fight Club,* starring Edward Norton and Brad Pitt, is projected on a wall.

While good movies are great at transporting you to another reality, there's nothing quite like 360 Screenings. The cinematic and theatrical experience designed by Loach and Gontier extends that feeling of escapism. "Ned and I always loved the unexplained territory," Gontier told me. "We lived in Europe together for a while, and there were really amazing artistic advances over there." In New York, they saw the play *Sleep No More,* for which audience members wear masks and chase the impeccably choreographed cast around different rooms in a seven-floor building. The performances happen simultaneously, so each audience member chooses his or her own adventure.

Captivated by the convergence of art and theater, the duo now brings hit cult movies to life, including *Fight Club, Amélie,* and *28 Days Later.* Loach described this to me as a fusion: "When there is a gap of opportunity in the artistic fabric, you can create something that hasn't been done before. People don't always know what they want, and by combining things you can create something remarkable."

Art, film, and drama are all popular industries, but each is littered with hundreds of failed companies. 360 Screenings layers real-life experiences onto existing movies. The concept converges the emotional tug of nostalgic pop culture movies, the rush of being swept up in a flash-mob-like movie scene, the interaction and control of video games, and the deep psychological attraction of a mystery. The public seems hungry for the experience. "We were worried the audience would be too timid to fully experience everything," Gontier explained to me. "But our audiences are prepared to dig and take things to the next level."

LAYERING IMMERSION

The practice of layering on immersion experiences is increasingly popular in a range of businesses and industries. Over 100,000 British fans recently rushed to join an IKEA Facebook page, hoping for the chance to spend the night in one of the company's gigantic stores. One hundred pajama-clad patrons were invited to the IKEA sleepover party for a night of camping in their showroom while being treated to movies and spa services.

In another example, the cable channel TNT found a sleepy little Belgium town where not too much happens and placed a pedestal in the center of the town square. On the pedestal was a conspicuous button with a meek little sign that read, "Push to Add Drama." When an innocent bicyclist finally pressed the mysterious button, a live, adrenaline-fueled fight broke out in the street, followed by a mysterious woman on a motorcycle, a car chase, and a bloody shoot-out. The bizarre series of action-packed events ended with the reveal of a giant banner on a nearby building that read, "Your Daily Dose of Drama—TNT." The intensity of TV-style action on city streets led to 50 million video views.

Immersion is likely to become an increasingly popular strategy. 360 Screenings, for instance, answers a wistful desire we all have for real life to be as exciting as what we see on the big screen—at least once in a while. Loach told me, "People love trying to figure it [the movie] out based on the clues." To fuel this excitement, 360 Screenings floods social media with cryptic clues to spur a movie-guessing game, inspiring movie fans and followers around the world to chime in with guesses.

In 360's first year, all six of Loach and Gontier's top-secret productions sold out, supported by $60 admission fees and five-dollar drinks. But you don't have to have multiple degrees in the arts to create a fully immersive experience for your customers—or, for that matter, for your colleagues and employees. It's a model that, with minor variations, is very replicable in any workplace or industry.

CONVERGENCE AT TREND HUNTER

At Trend Hunter, we've also noticed the problems with millennial underemployment, so we launched a training program called The Trend Hunter Academy. Our initial goal was to create a pipeline for new talent, but our approach has spiraled into a completely different way to approach work culture.

As a trend publication, we know from experience that our ideal worker is a young, digitally connected person with a passion for digital media. Digital media is poorly covered in traditional school programs, so few applicants are trained in what we need. There is a risk in hiring these young, inexperienced people. How do you find the most passionate among them and create an environment in which they and, in turn, the company can thrive?

It starts by considering what interests young professionals. While they might enjoy video games and beer, they truly thrive when they're given challenges. Motivated more by social achievements than by money, they crave new skills and qualifications. To satisfy all of these needs, while tapping into their preferred leisure activity, we created the ultimate workplace experiment in convergence.

From a design perspective, our office is perfectly suited to young professionals. It's a hip, 5,000-square-foot, brick-walled loft in Toronto's fashion district. Our furnishings are a blend of modern and retro, with 1960s bubble chairs, retro fridges, vintage typewriters, digital walls, and our very own bar.

Instead of holding dull office meetings, we put on beer parties, which involve individual work updates. Rather than employ traditional motivation tactics, we've created a video game–like system of reward, digitally projecting everyone's stats on our wall. To make sure new people are challenged, we try to publish their work within their first few days, and we push each person to try new projects, categories, and styles of writing. To satisfy their need for new qualifications, we'll run them through forty workshops and training sessions in just a few months, instructing them in interview technique, millennial stereotypes, and corporate professionalism. And at the program's end, we have a graduation ceremony that celebrates the millions of page views employees have attracted to their new writing portfolio.

To date, 4,000 people have applied to this program, our exclusive means for finding and hiring new employees. Along the way, I've learned that a millennial-friendly work environment requires a convergence of many different changes to the traditional workplace. By making these changes, we've seen some extraordinary improvements. Using the wall-projected dashboard alone, we were able to increase productivity by 80 percent. Our Friday beer parties have become weekly get-togethers that last until 10:00 p.m., and we've even added a monthly series of educational keynote videos that we call "Feel Smarter Fridays." The result? A happy, motivated workforce and a giant pool of potential future hires.

SUB-PATTERNS OF CONVERGENCE

As we've seen in this chapter, convergence can take many different forms. Here is a cheat sheet of all the forms and sub-patterns that you can explore to help you find better ideas and opportunities— and find them faster.

ALIGNING WITH MULTIPLE FORCES More than a decade ago, the scrappy start-up Method leaped into the cluttered market for bathroom soaps and cleaning agents, which was dominated by consumer packaged goods giants such as Unilever and Procter & Gamble (P&G). Method combined eco-friendly ingredients with design-centric packaging to create an overall vibe of sophistication. The extraordinary outcome: a line of cleaning products that soon racked up annual revenue of $100 million. Even more surprising was the impression the brand left on consumers, who were so taken with the elegance of the bottles that they often put them on display.

COMBINING PHYSICAL AND DIGITAL Webkinz became an international sensation by inventing a plush toy that keys into the digital world. Each toy includes a unique "secret code" that kids can use to unlock a virtual playroom containing the same character. By 2011, the company had taken in $100 million, and it quickly went on to generate hundreds of millions in sales.[5]

---

5   Jacob Ogles, "How to Take Money from Kids: Sell Toys Both Physical and Virtual," *Wired*, August 13, 2007, http://archive.wired.com/gadgets/miscellaneous/news/2007/07/webkinz?currentPage=all.

CONVERGING PEOPLE Convergence in our social media–driven world connects buyers and sellers around shared interests, ranging from the product-focused crowd-funding pioneered by KickStarter to the fan- and cause-based crowd-funding of IndieGoGo.

COMBINING BRANDS In 2005, Taiwanese-based EVA Air teamed up with Japan's Sanrio to launch a co-branded Hello Kitty cartoon-painted airplane. Critics predicted that it would be a short-lived marketing gimmick. A decade later, EVA is achieving record revenue with a fleet of Hello Kitty planes christened Happy Music Time, Speed Puff, and Hello Kitty Loves Apple. The colorfully designed planes have made flying fun, bridged culture gaps, occupied otherwise anxious kids, and even sparked interest in Japanese tourism.

ADDING VALUE OpenLabel took the bar code, a ubiquitous tool of retail, and fashioned a phone app that lets shoppers amplify their experience by quickly pulling up relevant nutritional information, recommendations, and coupons.

SUMMARY: CONVERGENCE

The diverse mix of individuals whom you met in this chapter—from Kyla Gutsche to Dave Dahl to Ned Loach and Robert Gontier—all profited by capitalizing on convergence. Kyla's tattoo business wouldn't have been possible without combining innovations in micro-pigmentation, prison tattoo techniques, and Titian's remarkable pigment layering. And whereas Dave's Killer Bread saw initial success from nothing more than a shocking label and a great recipe, it was Dahl's unexpected mix of seemingly unrelated hot trends—prison culture and organic, eco-friendly eating—that caused his business to soar to stratospheric heights. Finally, 360 Screenings juiced up traditional movie watching by layering on a theatrical experience, making the familiar new again.

TAKEAWAYS

1. **Chaos Creates Opportunity** Adversity can be liberating, because it frees us from the obligation of our set path, awakening our inner hunter. Kyla's innovations flourished when she was forced to find a new occupation.

2. **Multiply Your Odds of Success** By aligning with multiple trends, you can increase your reach and potential, capturing incremental customers and attention.

3. **Your Future May Dwell in the Past** New technologies and ideas often flourish by borrowing aspects of proven past ideas, creating ingenious products and services. Kyla developed a more advanced method to mimic human skin tones by reaching back to a Renaissance-era painter.

4. **Don't Ignore the Fringe** So-called establishment institutions often teach us that little value comes from the fringe, but outlaw culture and avant-garde culture often inspire great ideas.

5. **Combine to Create Something New** Marrying two ideas often yields something unexpectedly new, such as the many evolutions of GPS combinations. Search for concepts that can be woven together.

Chapter 6

DIVERGENCE

DIVERGENCE: Products and services designed to oppose or break free from the mainstream. This opportunity pattern extends beyond rebellion to include personalization, customization, status, and luxury.

M odern culture celebrates rebellious thinkers and counterintuitive ideas. We're psychologically predisposed to pay attention to what's different, whether it's Richard Branson's space program, American Apparel's controversial advertising, or the shocking stunts of the latest misbehaving musical sensation. But we all exhibit divergent thinking when we dance to the songs our parents hate, personalize our homes to reflect our quirky tastes, or choose the batman cuff links over the standard sterling silver.

The media demonstrates divergence in its celebration of the antihero, as seen on such television shows as *The Sopranos, 24, Weeds, House of Cards,* and *Breaking Bad.* These shows conflict with negative stereotypes by celebrating mobsters, a pot-pushing mom, a murderous congressman, and a meth-cooking high school teacher. Pay attention to these shows. They are more than entertainment. They signify a sharp cultural shift away from mainstream thinking, and they are a good map for how new business ideas take shape.

Over the last few decades, divergent opportunities have become more prevalent, fueled by the diversification of media, Internet culture, and technology. Today, it's hard to imagine the uniformity of the 1980s. Back then, almost everyone watched the same television show on Thursday night, craved the same Michael Jordan–branded shoe, and aspired to play the same sports and games. The Rubik's Cube, for example, sold 350 million units in the 1980s. That's astounding.

Today, people don't all want the same thing. They watch different shows, read different blogs, and crave unique products. Partly, this shift has taken place because of the Internet; partly, it's attributable to lower barriers to manufacturing and marketing niche consumer goods. Today, individualism is more highly prized than uniformity. For example, you can customize your own clothing online, personalize your own granola bars, and select dozens (if not hundreds) of options on your next car.

Divergence is one of the best tactics to employ when battling a giant. In the early 1980s, a Hollywood executive named Jay Stein decided he wanted to top Walt Disney's theme park. Most corporate executives would start by studying what makes a great theme park, such as family-friendly hospitality and all the psychological triggers that delight Disneyland tourists. Stein took a totally different tack. He reckoned that he couldn't beat Disney at its own game, so instead he studied how to scare, shock, and intimidate guests. This led him to create the loud, edgy, in-your-face Universal Studios Hollywood, a fist-pumping destination crammed full of adrenaline-rush adventures that family-friendly Disney would never offer. As Stein put it, "Every day there are customer complaints that the fireballs are too hot. The shark on the Jaws ride comes too close to the boat . . . and every day thousands of people come back for more."[1] If Disneyland were a cup of tea, Universal Studios would be a barrel of Red Bull.

The path of divergence is often blocked by hesitation, fear, and

---

1   Jordan DiPietro, "The Next Revolutionary Stock," *The Motley Fool*, May 7, 2010.

conservatism. Dare float a divergent idea, and it's likely a boss or friend will tell you that you're wildly off course and warn you to get back on that mainstream bus. In large companies, you'll probably face resistance and a gauntlet of rules, regulations, and legal compliance. In small firms, you may have a difficult time lining up investors and building critical mass.

For example, when Toyota introduced the hybrid Prius, gas-guzzling consumers laughed it off as an oddity, and almost a decade would pass before Toyota's strategy appeared brilliant. When Billy Bean proposed using analytics to recruit baseball players for the Oakland A's, team scouts feared disaster. They'd been entrusted for so long to deliver the *real* scoop on players that they couldn't imagine baseball being played by the numbers. But, of course, fans of Michael Lewis's *Moneyball* know that Bean's quantitative strategy forever changed the way the game is played.

There have always been similar setbacks for those who want to diverge. Rewind a few centuries and imagine a world under constant threat from untreatable disease—from leprosy to smallpox to influenza to black plague. Today, people may fear superbugs, but imagine how much more fear there would be without modern science. In the 1700s, people didn't expect miracle cures to be just around the corner, and if someone had a disease, you'd be best served to keep your distance. In 1796, Edward Jenner, an English physician, gained fame by rejecting that tradition with his wild notion that scabs and pus from infected people should be ingested, snorted, and rubbed into non-infected patients. His brave experimentation led to the world's first modern vaccines. A new era of health care was born, but for this to happen, Jenner needed to overcome orthodoxy.

By dissecting and diverging from successful ideas, you can find incredible opportunity.

SUBTLE GESTURES AND THE BEAUTY OF UGLINESS

How do you attract the attention of the woman sitting next to you? That was the challenge for David Horvath, a young art student sitting through illustration class at Parsons New School for Design. His quest was complicated by the day's task: sketching the shapely nude woman who was posing just a few feet away. Sketching another woman—naked, no less—didn't seem like a great setting to first approach the girl of his dreams.

Instead, Horvath rebelled. While Sun-Min Kim, the object of his affection, was meticulously capturing the model's elegant lines, Horvath mocked up an ugly, cartoonish character in the same pose. His quirky beast was a squat, bucktoothed, googly-eyed monster with peculiarly tiny hands and feet.

The professor was not impressed, calling his drawing "ugly" and "hideous."

Horvath explained to me that he shot back: "Ugly is the new beautiful!"

Kim was impressed by his wit. She smiled and said, "That was interesting. I like what you just said right there," which in art-student code translates to "I kind of like you." And just like that, an ugly little doodled creature sparked a connection between two blushing artists.

Over the next few weeks, Horvath and Kim's illustrated flirtation grew into a budding relationship. They shared a mutual vision of ugly little characters, worlds away from today's sugarcoated status quo. Rejecting Barbie doll perfection and wide-shouldered knights in shining armor, they imagined an inverse reality of misfit characters with wonky eyes, droopy ears, and buckteeth.

At the time, the two were merely exploring curiosities, bonding over shared ideals. They didn't imagine that they might be laying the blueprint for a business. Then came the twist: Upon graduation,

Kim's student visa expired and she was forced to return home to Korea.

Faced with the risk of losing his love, Horvath began courting Kim with handwritten love letters, each signed with a drawing of Wage, the ugly little character that had brought them together. Simultaneously awkward and adorable, the bloated little hairless orange monster had beady, far-set eyes and a curiously blank, gap-toothed expression.

Horvath's drawings began to win Kim's heart. By Christmas, Kim bought some colorful orange felt and attempted her first sewn craft—a crudely stitched doll version of Wage, which she sent to Horvath from Korea.

Thousands of miles away in New York, Horvath opened his present and was delighted. Kim's lovingly hand-crafted creation was a metaphoric trophy—tangible proof that she loved him back.

Horvath explained to me that he showed off the doll to a friend, who shocked him with his reaction: "Great! I'll take twenty!" His friend, also a lover of art, owned Giant Robot, a Japanese pop-culture shop. A thrilled Kim hand-stitched twenty more, and the $30 dolls were all snapped up on the first day. Giant Robot ordered forty more, which sold out in two days. Horvath penned a biography for Wage, and he started imagining more characters—Babo, Jeero, Wedgehead, and Ice-Bat, each with their own stories.

Kim began churning out several dolls a day. The weeks turned into months. A year and a half later, she wrote to Horvath: "I've made 1,500 of these things and my fingers are blue and red. We are either going to have to stop or do this for real."

She was right, of course, but how do you gain distribution for a weird, one-of-a-kind doll? Horvath's first step was counterintuitive. He ignored the big retailers. He knew they'd likely impose rules that would dull the uniqueness of his creations, forcing his dolls to conform. His distribution strategy would need to be as divergent as his doll.

Horvath set out on an exhausting hunt up and down hundreds of streets and avenues in New York City, seeking out quirky little stores, boutiques, jewelry stores, and museum shops that he hoped would be intrigued. It worked. Buyers were captivated. "They saw it as more than just a line of plush dolls," he said, explaining to me that what customers were attracted to was the story.

Within the year, the couple reconnected at the New York Toy Fair, and they were soon engaged. But the wedding had to wait. The national publicity tour came first, and they went on the road, living in hotels and investing every last dollar into their launch. By late 2005, their product, Uglydolls, could be purchased from an astonishing 2,500 locations. The dolls were a hit, especially with boys who typically don't play with dolls. But Uglydolls were different, with their mismatched eyes, tongues that stick out, sharp little teeth, and sinister names, such as Ox, Ice-Bat, Sour Corn, and Puglee.

The creatures were also snapped up by such celebrity collectors as Snoop Dogg, Nelly, Nicole Richie, Ashlee Simpson, and Sasha Obama. The dolls sported cameos in half a dozen feature films and were featured in art exhibits around the world, including the Louvre, home of the *Mona Lisa*. By 2012, the dolls and accessories were generating more than $100 million in annual revenue.

The quirky dolls tapped into a powerful and authentic backlash against impossible standards of beauty. During the same period, Trend Hunter spotted this happening in many different realms. We were covering numerous stories of beauty rebellion, such as the Ugly Model Agency, magazine covers without Photoshop, Awkward Family Photos, ugly Christmas sweater parties, and even dating sites for people who declare themselves as less attractive.

There's always some degree of rebellion against the mainstream, but when you see signs of backlash, it's worth investigating the potential of divergent ideas. In 2004, Unilever picked up on the "female beauty backlash" and began funding research that would transform its Dove soap brand. Incredibly, the research revealed that only 2 percent of women believe they're beautiful. In response, the company launched the Campaign for Real Beauty. In one of the most successful ad campaigns of the decade, Dove exposed the extreme photo manipulation that goes into creating a billboard ad, setting up an implicit contrast by featuring unaltered images of real women.

This was only the beginning of Dove's campaign to celebrate diversity in appearance. In 2013, Unilever underlined its point by hiring FBI sketch artists to draw women based first on how they describe themselves and second on how they're described by others. The video campaign that sprung from this experiment dramatically illustrated how critical some women are of their own appearance. The video, translated into multiple languages, captured over 100 million YouTube views in a single month—at that point the most viral video ad ever.

David Horvath has had time to think deeply about the lessons behind his success. "Do what you love to do," he told me. When shaping your creative vision, he said, it helps to close your eyes to the mainstream. "Don't try to look at what anyone else is doing. You can easily fall into the trap of looking at the hot thing and trying to replicate it. You're never going to get a breakthrough. If you follow your competitors, you're always going to be behind them on the path. You need to push out and find your own way."

UGLY LESSONS APPLIED

As I reflected on Horvath's advice, I thought about a challenge I was then confronting. After dating my girlfriend, Shelby, for several years, I was eagerly looking for a memorable way to propose. However, as a Trend Hunter, I knew I'd have to attempt something extraordinarily creative. Uglydoll gave me an idea. I ordered an orange monster named Crazymonster and a pink monster named Wippy, and I then staged the pair in a series of photos throughout Toronto. In fifty images or so, I re-created the story of how Shelby and I met and fell in love.

Next, on a keynote trip to Monaco, I'd booked us a table at the Vista Palace perched up against a window overlooking the Mediterranean coastline. As Shelby looked through the menu, I pulled out my smuggled Uglydoll photos and narrated the story of our relationship. As the photo shoot scenes became more recognizable, I neared my big question. "In case you can't tell, Shelby, this story is about us!"

"Shelby, will you marry me?"

To my delight, she said yes. If you're romantically curious, you can find my hidden video footage by searching for "Ugly Dolls Proposal" on Google or YouTube.

THE PURSUIT OF COOL

At Trend Hunter, we've always maintained that popular isn't cool. The pursuit of cool is about something cutting-edge and unique. "Don't chase after the hot thing," David Horvath said. "If it's hot, somebody has already done it. You have to come up with something from scratch."[2]

How can you learn to try for something radical? The first step is to not fear the outcome. "You need to push yourself to go out on your own," Horvath told me. There's a leap of faith with divergence. It's the opposite of painting by the numbers. There are no numbers. And sometimes there's no paint. "You have to really *do* it," Horvath said. "Not just talk about it."

---

2   Sarah E. Needleman, "A Love Letter Begets Dolls," *Wall Street Journal,* December 19, 2012, http://online.wsj.com/article/SB10001424127887324907204578187510 242227022.html.

Another key lesson here is that truly divergent ideas market themselves. Specific clusters of customers are often excited by points of difference and imperfection, which generates turbo power out of the gate. "We never did any marketing or advertising," said Horvath. "When you're different, people talk about you, and that creates a more authentic love."

Uglydoll is a potent example of how rebelling against conventional, mainstream thoughts and beliefs can spark a whole range of divergent patterns, including radical approaches to product design, marketing, and distribution. It's also proof that by identifying what's popular and then going against it, you can find or create something truly cool.

LAWSUITS, RUMORS, AND JET RACING

You probably already know something about Red Bull. You know the cans are absurdly small, the drink is ridiculously expensive, and it tastes like cough medicine. You might even know about the company's sponsorship of ice racing, cliff diving, parachuting from space, jet racing, and freestyle motocross.

But you've probably never heard of the Red Bull's secretive past and its carefully designed strategy of divergence. It's a tale that begins with young daredevil Dietrich Mateschitz, a fun-loving, fast-skiing Austrian rebel with an infectious, cheek-to-cheek smile and rugged good looks. Mateschitz loved everything about college life except perhaps the studying, and he took an astounding ten years to finish his marketing degree at Vienna University.

After a decade of steep slopes and late nights, Mateschitz graduated to a job promoting detergent for Unilever. He worked his way up the ladder, and he ended up at Blendax, a toothpaste maker later acquired by P&G. Mateschitz was earning a top salary and travelling the globe, but how excited can you get about toothpaste? And just like that, he realized that he'd blown a decade selling house-hold products.

Years later, he'd tell *Businessweek* that he'd hit a wall: "All I could see was the same gray airplanes, the same gray suits, the same gray faces . . . I asked myself whether I wanted to spend the next decade as I'd spent the previous one."[3]

On one of his frequent jet-lagged business trips to Thailand, Mateschitz stumbled upon a medicinal concoction more elevating than coffee. Krating Daeng triggered alertness and concentration, making it a favorite stimulant for sleep-deprived Thai cabdrivers. Loosely translated, the name meant "red water buffalo." Mateschitz was soon hooked, knocking back half a dozen red water buffaloes a day.

He immediately recognized the marketing opportunity and began pitching the drink's original creator, a Thai businessman named Chaleo Yoovidhya. Mateschitz wanted to turn the drink into a global brand, but there was a catch: The drink *tasted* awful.

Over the next year, the two removed a few ingredients and added carbonation to mask the harsh flavor, but the concoction still tasted horrible. Mateschitz realized a much different marketing path would be needed. "It's not just another flavored sugar water differentiated by color or taste or flavor," he later explained to *Businessweek*. "It's an efficiency product. I'm talking about improving endurance, concentration, reaction time, speed, vigilance, and emotional status. Taste is of no importance whatsoever."[4]

The water buffalo drink would be marketed as Red Bull. Instead of focusing on taste, Mateschitz and Yoovidhya would celebrate the

---

3   Duff McDonald, "Red Bull's Billionaire Maniac," *Bloomberg Businessweek,* May 19, 2011, http://www.businessweek.com/magazine/content/11_22/b4230064852768 .htm.

4   Duff McDonald, "Red Bull's Billionaire Maniac," *Bloomberg Businessweek,* May 18, 2011, http://www.businessweek.com/stories/2011-05-18/red-bulls-billionaire -maniac.

lifestyle of the drink's hard-charging aficionados. The two entrepreneurs honed the concept and then tested it with focus groups. It didn't go well. "I'd never before experienced such a disaster," Mateschitz told *Forbes*. "People didn't believe the taste, the logo, the brand name."[5]

But Mateschitz and Yoovidhya were undaunted. They knew that they needed a nonconventional marketing strategy. Mateschitz brought his counterintuitive beliefs to his college pal, Johannes Kastner, who'd founded an ad agency in Frankfurt six years earlier. Kastner agreed that the brown, syrupy concoction tasted "nasty," but he took on the challenge. Kastner & Partners intentionally marketed Red Bull to be subversive.[6] There'd be no traditional brand merchandising. The drink would be nonconformist, self-ironic, and polarizing.

Pricing would be intentionally outrageous (three to six times the price of a Coke), helping to separate Red Bull from the competition while exuding mystery. The drink wouldn't target a demographic; it would be marketed to a "state of mind." The campaign began with a simple slogan: "Red Bull gives you wings."

While the plan got the drink rolling, it was just stage one. Over a couple of beers with Hans Vriens, Red Bull's third employee, I learned more about what really took Red Bull over the top. Vriens, who is currently the innovation chief at Hershey's, explained that Red Bull wasn't so much a drink as a divergent brand message buoyed by rumors and intrigue. It was this divergence that gave the company its momentum.

In 1996, Vriens's North American Red Bull launch budget was a paltry $2.5 million, a fraction of the $50 to $100 million normally required for a national launch. But Vriens hoped to generate

5   Kerry A. Dolan, "The Soda with Buzz," *Forbes,* March 28, 2005, http://www .forbes.com/global/2005/0328/028.html.

6   Kastner & Partners, "Red Bull: A Success Story," http://kastnerandpartners.com.

buzz through other avenues. Urban myths or rumors can spread like wildfire, and they cost virtually nothing. You may have heard the bull balls rumor—the peculiar idea that taurine, Red Bull's mystery ingredient, is extracted from bull testicles. That nutty concept appeals to testosterone-charged males, but it's false. While a traditional corporation might issue a press release correction, Red Bull built an unmoderated fan site, which essentially functioned as a rumor mill. The company knew that when fans imagine your energy drink has phenomenal, mystical ingredients, that's a rumor you want to run wild.

Mateschitz summarized his unconventional strategy in *Business-week*: "In the beginning, the high-school teachers who were against the product were at least as important as the students who were for it. . . . Newspapers asked, 'Is it a drug? Is it harmless? Is it dangerous?'"[7]

Authority figures who railed against Red Bull only fanned the flames, making the mysterious drink seem just as alluring as other pursuits youths are unsuccessfully warned against—sex, drugs, and rock 'n' roll. The opposition handed the divergent product free advertising. The more they railed against it, the more Red Bull sold. After all, few things are more attractive to a young person than something prohibited by adults (for example, there's compelling evidence that Nancy Reagan's "Just Say No" campaign actually *increased* drug usage by making young people aware of drugs they had previously known nothing about).

Just as the first wave of rumors was giving Red Bull badly needed traction, Mateschitz became even more mysterious. The inner workings of the company seemed impenetrable. Mateschitz became a reclusive enigma, known within the company as the Yeti. At first glance, this seems bizarre, but the company was crafting an

---

7 Duff McDonald, "Red Bull's Billionaire Maniac," *Bloomberg Business-week*, May 18, 2011, http://www.businessweek.com/stories/2011-05-18/red-bulls-billionaire-maniac.

image based on mystery, and it was only fitting that Mateschitz's leadership also reflected its share of intrigue.

But then the rebellious drink encountered a different kind of obstacle when there was a drunk-driving accident involving teenagers who had mixed Red Bull with vodka. The incident spurred public outcry to remove Red Bull from shelves. Officials were pushing for a ban, arguing that mixing the stimulant with alcohol was dangerous. Red Bull's lawyers responded with a potent counterargument that Vriens paraphrased to me as, "Sure, you can ban Red Bull. But then you should also ban the other drinks people are mixing with vodka, like orange juice and Coca-Cola." Obviously, that wasn't going to happen, but the point was made clear. The government responded by asking if Red Bull would at least put on a warning label while the drink was further investigated.

"A warning label?" Vriens retold the story with excitement. "You bet. And what would you like that warning label to say?" First, they asked that the beverage be labeled "not for teenagers." "Yes," he explained. "What else?" Next, they said it shouldn't be used by pregnant women. "That's like telling them you can prove this stuff works!" And finally, they asked Red Bull to suggest the drink shouldn't be mixed with vodka. It was like putting the recipe on the bottle.

Vriens points out that crude government attempts to regulate Red Bull only fueled an already red-hot brand, generated free publicity, and enhanced its appeal. Sales of Red Bull exploded.

At Trend Hunter, we've consistently seen that consumers are drawn to the thrill of what we call "shockvertising" and "danger marketing." For example, readers have been disproportionately excited by articles on monster fashion, terror apparel, and charitable shockvertising. We've covered dozens of charities that have ditched the typical sympathy pull in favor of more head-turning strategies: fake dead bodies, nudity, and so on. Danger marketing gets attention.

Fifteen years after it was launched, Red Bull has expanded into a $15 billion empire, captain of its own category and icon of late-night partygoers. Next, Red Bull Media promises to venture where no beverage company has gone before, expanding into television, print, and music.

Red Bull teaches the viral potential of rebellion, but it also demonstrates that you don't need perfection if your positioning is boldly unique. Remarkably, an awful taste and high price actually seemed to help substantiate Red Bull's lofty claims.

If you're exploring a concept that differs from the mainstream, it can be useful to examine your weaknesses to consider whether you can position them as points of differentiation. For Red Bull, the unpleasant flavor played well with the drink's purported near-medicinal quality.

Finally, Red Bull teaches that you can tap into people's inner desire to be different. What's beautiful about that sentiment is that today, there are many more strands of difference than ever before, a truth that becomes even clearer in our next story.

BEAUTIFUL PEOPLE ONLY

Robert Hintz lost his job at a Denmark radio station and then lost his apartment. But he hadn't lost his interest in the opposite sex, and he had plenty of time on his hands. He decided to sign up for a dating site.

He thought he was just looking for a date, but he was actually hunting for his next business idea. He told me, "When you hit the bottom, your brain starts working like a survivor searching for a way out."

While searching for a match, Hintz found himself thinking about the online process. He considered himself a good-looking guy, and he quickly spotted an attractive woman. But there was a problem. Her profile was already inundated by other suitors. He sympathized with her predicament. "I realized she'd received 500-plus messages from guys who were probably far from her match. So the chance that she might find her ideal mate would be difficult."

That simple but insightful observation inspired Hintz to think about a different kind of dating site. "What if members of the opposite sex could vote you in?" he wondered. He felt he was onto something, and his search was given added urgency by the fact that he was "broke and living in a tent."

As Hintz explored his idea, he saw that many sites allowed searches for eye and hair color. Technically, those search features might help you find someone whom you find attractive, but at some level, they all seemed to dance around why people frequent online dating sites. If physical attraction was so important, why not create a site that catered specifically to that need? He named his new idea Beautiful People. "I wanted to make sure there was a controversial business idea and news story," he said. "I was betting that something focused and provocative would get media attention."

Hintz was exploiting a valid, marketable insight: Online daters rarely confess that they're primarily guided by superficial tendencies. Yet research suggests that physical attraction is the most popular deciding factor for online daters. In Hintz's view, the billion-dollar online dating business was overlooking our superficial, biologically driven tendencies. Though we may no longer be searching for hips suitable for childbearing or shoulders ideal for killing prey, we are still strongly driven by physical attraction. Instead of dancing around the truth, Hintz blueprinted an openly elitist dating site that would jump straight to physical attraction. It would be the most (or least, depending on how you look at it) pretentious and controversial dating site in the world.

Unfortunately, the market for online dating was already saturated. If Hintz had paid a business expert to weigh his chances, the expert might have told him he was better off going back to the radio station to ask for his job back. In 2001, several million visitors were already flocking to the billion-dollar dating site blockbusters OKCupid, eHarmony.com, LavaLife.com, PlentyOFish.com, and Match.com. During that year, more than 10 percent of Americans stated that they'd met their partners online, a figure that would double by 2007 and triple by 2013.[8]

Competing against these well-financed mainstream companies seemed impossible. So Hintz prototyped a simple, beauty-based dating site in tiny Denmark, and, strangely enough, it worked. The success of that prototype led to the brand BeautifulPeople.com, which soon achieved global expansion. His friend Greg Hodge—also dashingly handsome—would become the site's managing director and spokesperson. "Like it or hate it . . . we all want to be with someone we are attracted to," Hodge would later explain. "People who claim otherwise are lying. I am beautiful, my wife is beautiful and my baby daughter is beautiful. I make no apologies for it."[9]

As Beautiful People expanded to other countries, Hodge sought out the most sensational national publications and planted controversial ideas like brush fires. "I'd feed them titles like 'Ugly People Forbidden,'" he told me. "They would see the fire and get hooked."

BeautifulPeople.com soon became a dating site like no other. Existing members act like the doorman at a hot New York City club. Every day, thousands of applicants submit their photos, and four out of five are summarily rejected. Millions have been rejected, a fact BeautifulPeople.com trumpets. Hodge was clear about his marketing task. "You need to be exclusive to a community, and in

---

8   Eli J. Finkel, Paul W. Eastwick, Benjamin R. Karney, Harry T. Reis, and Susan Sprecher, "Online Dating: A Critical Analysis From the Perspective of Psychological Science," Association for Psychological Science, 2012.

9   Greg Hodge, "Forgive Them, for They Know Not What Is Gay," *Huffington Post Gay Voices*, July 31, 2012, http://www.huffingtonpost.com/greg-hodge/beautifulpeople-gay-marriage_b_1724382.html.

our case, instead of playing that down, we run with it and embrace it," Hodge explained to me. "The cornerstone to our success is that authenticity and controversy—it sparks debate."

If you find this a bit offensive, you're not alone. In the site's early days, blogs and newspapers were up in arms. But Hodge went on the offensive, giving the media exactly what it seemed to want: a politically incorrect, devilishly handsome villain.

Divergent tactics spark headlines, and Hodge carved out divergence with abandon. In 2006, he began releasing unabashedly politically incorrect Beautiful People approval-rate statistics. *The Telegraph* ate it up with a headline that ignited a flood of coverage: "British people among world's ugliest, according to Beautifulpeople .com."[10]

When the site went global in the fall of 2009, it issued a press wire release: "1.8 million Ugly People Turned Away Over Two Weeks, as BeautifulPeople.com Goes Global."[11] The release nakedly contrasted two "ugly" nations—Great Britain and Germany—to "beautiful" Sweden, Brazil, and Norway.

The in-your-face marketing led to a flurry of articles and hundreds of thousands of new members. In 2012, Hodge rode the gay marriage movement, with the advertised launch of Beautiful People Gay and Beautiful Women Only. The clamorous negative attention attracted millions to BeautifulPeople.com, and soon dozens of corporate sponsors saw the site as an ideal community for launching new products, events, and clubs. The intentional divergence led to

---

10 "British People Among World's Ugliest, According to BeautifulPeople.com," November 11, 2009, *Telegraph* (London), http://www.telegraph.co.uk/women/ sex/6542263/British-people-among-worlds-ugliest-according-to-BeautifulPeople .com.html.

11 "1.8 million Ugly People Turned Away Over Two Weeks, as BeautifulPeople .com Goes Global" Press Release on PR Newswire, November 10, 2009, http:// www.prnewswire.com/news-releases/18-million-ugly-people-turned-away-over-two -weeks-as-beautifulpeoplecom-goes-global-69641767.html.

750,000 paying members, which spawned an additional business: Beautiful People Jobs. Talent agencies had already been trolling the site for reality TV cast members, and Hodge made it official, announcing that many of his prequalified beautiful members were available for hire.

While it's easy to attack Beautiful People for its arguably exclusionary and insensitive approach, focusing on appearances has been a successful strategy, judging by the half-dozen hugely popular iPhone and Android hook-up apps, such as Tinder, which caught fire in September of 2012 at a USC party. Astonishingly, all the sex app does is show users a photo and a brief description: Swipe right to begin the hook-up. Swipe left to say no. Today, the service has 2 million members.

THE PROLIFERATION OF NICHE IDEALS

A wholesome matchmaking alternative to Beautiful People and Tinder is Joe Shapira's JDate, the Jewish-only dating site that is also a divergent hit. When JDate hit $70 million in revenue in 2004, the company launched into massive, shotgun-style corporate divergence, broadening into thirty niche dating communities, including Faith.com, Christian Mingle, Military Singles, Deaf Singles, Interracial Singles, and Black Singles. Other entrepreneurs have also successfully played the divergent dating card by creating niche sites, including Date My Dog (a site for passionate dog-lovers), Positive Singles (for singles living with STDs), Green Singles (for eco-friendly people), Gluten Free Date (for those with celiac disease), We Waited (for virgins), Senior People Meet (for Grandpa), 420 Dating (for marijuana lovers), and Till Death Do Us Part (for terminally ill singles).

The explosion of niche dating sites has also sparked opportunity for entrepreneurs who are looking to change in-person hook-ups. Companies specialize in group dating, "bus" dating, silent speed dating, Skype dating, and, yes, infidelity dating. The Ashley Madison infidelity dating service, which facilitates both random hook-ups and long-term relationships for married people looking to cheat, is so popular—over 21 million anonymous members—that it generates more than $60 million in revenue per year.

The common denominator is that these businesses have all flowed from divergent niche opportunities. And, significantly, these massive, multimillion-dollar opportunities were ripe for the taking for several years *after* the initial few mainstream sites launched and appeared to dominate. Today, niche online dating is a billion-dollar industry and provides an object lesson in the difference between seeing and truly observing. Just as beauty is in the eye of the beholder, there is often a lot more room to start a new venture if you have the foresight and boldness to break from the mainstream.

THE ARCHETYPE OF A DIVERGENT THINKER

Divergence is innate. Children, with their openness to serendipity and love of play, are naturally gifted at spotting divergent patterns. A famous study, asking how many uses a paper clip can be put to, showed that most adults can only fathom ten or fifteen. Kindergarteners can dream up 200. Unfortunately, those abilities quickly atrophy with education and age.[12]

Why? Well, for one, your chosen occupation or avocation often influences your skill at seeing divergent patterns. Researchers in Poland recently put sixty visual artists and sixty bank officers through tests of temperament and divergent thinking. Not surprisingly, *Scientific American* reported that the bank officers were average and the

---

12 Kamran Abbasi, "A Riot of Divergent Thinking," *Journal of the Royal Society of Medicine,* October 2011, http://www.ncbi.nlm.nih.gov/pmc/articles/PMC3184540.

artists "were amazingly good at flexibly generating original pictures and words."[13]

Bank officers are perhaps rightly prized for being conservative, for not taking chances—for *not* being divergent. That may be fine for managing your financial assets, but not for coming up with promising new business ideas. No matter your profession or passion, divergence is about thinking more like an artist than a banker.

THE SWEET TASTE OF DIVERGENCE

Food is one category in which most people push themselves to experience something new—new flavors, new restaurants, new bars, and so on. It can thus be a breeding ground for divergent thinking.

Several years ago, food truck cuisine was considered fit only for day laborers. Then, on a trip to Japan, Matt Cohen spotted something intriguing: Street vendors would serve up dishes cooked in the back of their trucks. The food was just as tasty and was served at a fraction of a sit-down restaurant's price. To bring this concept to America, Cohen held an event he called Off the Grid, bringing food trucks and live music to San Francisco's Fort Mason Center. The 2010 event was an instant hit, and today, fifteen food truck markets run weekly in the Bay Area. Moreover, within two years, the food truck craze spread across North America, becoming a new, less capital-intensive track for up-and-coming chefs to get their start.

Divergent opportunities may seem small at first, but the trick is to carve out niches with potential. In my client work, I use these examples to emphasize the power of creating ideas that are irre-

---

13 Scott Barry Kaufman, "How Do Artists Differ from Banker Officers?," *Scientific American*, June 15, 2013, http://blogs.scientificamerican.com/beautiful-minds/2013/06/15/how-do-artists-differ-from-bank-officers.

sistible to a specific group of people. Target everyone, and you're essentially targeting no one. Companies often fall into the trap of thinking that their products or services will reap the most benefit if they appeal to a broad market. That thinking often leads to generic creations that don't generate love from any particular group. To get a better feeling for how to avoid this trap, imagine for a minute that you're starting an ice cream business. Naturally, some of your initial choices will revolve around flavor. Vanilla would seem to be a good choice, as research suggests it's the most popular flavor. The problem is that consumers generally don't care whose vanilla ice cream they buy. They might buy one brand today and another tomorrow.

But if you love Ben & Jerry's Cherry Garcia, no other ice cream will do. The Vermont company launched its luxury flavor in 1991 in the midst of a global economic downturn. Surprising all the experts, in that same tough year, Cherry Garcia helped the company quadruple its sales. A decade later, the brand was acquired by Unilever for $326 million. In the words of the musician Jerry Garcia himself, "You do not merely want to be considered just the best of the best. You want to be considered the only ones who do what you do."[14]

SUB-PATTERNS OF DIVERGENCE

COUNTERCULTURE For decades, peppy Mountain Dew has flourished by countering the mainstream. The name itself, slang for moonshine, is pretty darn rebellious. While hard work was heralded in postwar 1950s America, contrarian Mountain Dew ads celebrated the country bumpkin who could always out-slick city folk. In the 1980s, as society largely embraced corporate America, Mountain

---

14 Warren Bennis and Patricia Ward Biederman, *Organizing Genius: The Secrets of Creative Collaboration.* New York: Basic Books, 1997.

Dew ads reacted by showing carefree skateboarders, rebelliously cruising by gray-suited business drones. While the 1990s spawned mega endorsement deals for Michael Jordan and other stars, Mountain Dew diverged from this trend with authentic ads featuring unnamed athletes playing sports for the love of the game.

PERSONALIZATION Every year in Australia, more than 100,000 dogs are euthanized because nobody wants to adopt them. Diverging from the traditional models for pet adoption shelters, Mars Petcare created an app called Dog-A-Like. The app exploits the popular belief that people already look like their canines by scanning photos of potential owners and searching their database of abandoned dogs to find a four-legged match. It was hugely popular, becoming the number one downloaded app in the Australia iTunes store, and saved thousands of dogs through a 13 percent rise in adoptions.

CUSTOMIZATION While personalization creates products specifically made for a given individual, customization is about giving him or her a higher-than-normal degree of choice. Nike, for example, launched the NikeID shoe, which enables athletes to customize nine different attributes, from the color of the laces to the color of the swoosh. Nike earned over $100 million from NikeID shoes in its first year of existence.

STATUS Although we tend to associate the word "divergence" with counterculture, the concept applies to all aspects of rejecting the mainstream status quo. Accordingly, the divergent pattern also explains our desire for luxury, notoriety, and status. In 1998, Nokia launched Vertu, a line of luxury mobile phones ranging from $5,000 to $310,000. Functionally, they aren't very different from the latest smartphone, but their gold, diamond, and leather accents have made them status symbols among the world's elite. In 2012,

Nokia sold the brand to a private equity firm, noting that Vertu revenues for the year would surpass $400 million.

STYLE In a desire to dress up our homes, vehicles, and favorite products, people purchase all sorts of accessories, ranging from covers for their phones to little Ping-Pong balls for their car antennas. One company, Antenna Balls, launched a full line of antenna balls, shaped like happy faces, 8-balls, and even cowgirls. Today, Antenna Balls sells half a million balls a month.

EXCLUSIVE BELONGING From club memberships to frequent-flyer rewards, the idea of exclusive belonging is to intentionally cater to a select group. In 1996, Greg Koch and Steve Wagner started Stone Brewing Company, a brewery most famous for its Arrogant Bastard Ale. The stronger brews were designed for beer connoisseurs and were generally not enjoyed by the mass market. To trumpet that differentiation, the company created the slogan "This is an aggressive beer. You probably won't like it." Stone's T-shirts are equally exclusionary, brandishing statements such as "Fizzy yellow beer is for wussies." Yet all that attitude has created a business that generates $100 million per year, with minimal advertising.

GENERATIONAL REBELLION Recent history continues to demonstrate that teenagers seek to distinguish themselves from their parents by pursuing radically different music, fashion, language, and hobbies. In the 1960s, Elvis and The Beatles were considered rebellious, just as Kanye West and Rihanna are considered rebellious in the 2010s. The only consistent aspect of teenage rebellion is this "not like my parents" urge.

FASHIONIZATION Many everyday products have thrived by diverging from the expected design. Examples include Karl Lagerfeld–branded

Diet Coke, Dita Von Teese–branded Perrier, and Voss water. Of particular interest is Voss, which in 2007 took the dull bottled-water industry by storm with a fashion-forward bottle design. The simple cylinder design and minimalist font helped the company grow its revenue to $140 million in its first four years.[15] Who would have expected that something as simple as a water bottle could become a fashion-oriented product?

SUMMARY: DIVERGENCE

In this chapter, we've seen how numerous entrepreneurs spearheaded highly original and extremely lucrative businesses by rejecting the well-beaten path. Uglydoll became a phenomenon without advertising or marketing because the doll's design diverged with our culture's artificial standards of beauty. Even the sales strategy was unconventional—ignoring traditional, big-box toy stores and selling straight to tiny, quirky boutiques. Meanwhile, Red Bull pioneered new territory by equating a beverage with a state of mind, adopting a radically divergent approach to pricing and marketing.

TAKEAWAYS

1. **Popular and Cool Are Different** Too often, people mistakenly pursue what's already popular. Popular is mainstream. It's crowded with competitors and, crucially, it's something that has already happened. Competitive advantage comes from searching for something cool, which is effectively the next big thing.

---

15 Natalie Zmuda, "Behind the Campaign: Voss Breaks First Major Consumer Push," *Advertising Age*, June 1, 2011, http://adage.com/article/news/campaign-voss -breaks-major-consumer-push/227862.

2. **Identify the Mainstream (to Repel It)** Increasingly, people are expecting products and services that reflect their unique personalities. There's a natural desire to diverge from the mainstream. For example, by taking the less popular route, UglyDoll differentiated itself as art and personal expression.

3. **Be Irresistible to a Specific Group of People** Invoke deep passion in one group. BeautifulPeople.com offends many people, but to those who love it, the following is cult-like. Remember, your product does not need to test well with everyone.

4. **Your Greatest Weakness Can Be Your Greatest Strength** Red Bull became one of the most successful beverages in the world despite tasting horrible, proving that not everything has to be perfect and that disadvantage can be remarketed into advantage.

Chapter 7

CYCLICALITY

↺

CYCLICALITY: Predictably recurring opportunities. Includes: retro, nostalgia, economic cycles, seasonality, generational patterns, and repetitive cycles.

The giant sea turtle appears to meander the Pacific in what seems like a carefree, slow-floating path of randomness. However, over the course of nearly two years, it repeats a 12,000-mile migration pattern. This epic pilgrimage always ends where it began: the exact beach where the mighty reptile was born. Over the course of its century-long life, this creature of habit will repeat its predictable journey fifty times.

What the sea turtle's wanderings teach us is that if you're too focused on the short-term meandering, you might fail to see the longer-term predictable pattern.

Consider for a moment what we can learn about cyclical opportunities from *Mad Men*'s Don Draper. Confident to a fault, Draper sways men and women alike with his charisma and rugged good looks. He exudes a level of power and influence that celebrates the heart of the 1960s golden era of advertising. When AMC launched *Mad Men*—with its very watchable characters smoking, drinking, fornicating, and pitching products—its huge popularity helped usher into pop culture a love for the era.

How did *Mad Men*'s producers know that a show set in the

1960s would be alluring? Why not a different era? Cyclical patterns seem obvious *after* they've taken effect, but to spot opportunities in advance, hunters need to constantly be on the lookout. They need to obsess about connecting the dots.

Mad Men's creator and producer, Matthew Weiner, wrote the script without a studio in 2000, but it would take another seven years to convince Hollywood execs that the timing for a 1960s show was just right. By 2007, fashion labels and designers were already celebrating the bright colors, bold patterns, clean lines, and irresistible curves of the 1960s. Remarkably, however, there were no modern adaptations of shows based on the 1960s on prime-time television.

By filling the 1960s TV gap, *Mad Men* fast-tracked itself for success. It was able to lay claim to a vast array of cultural themes, including civil rights, racism, women in the workplace, alcoholism, and, of course, sex, drugs, and rock 'n' roll. It wasn't just that *Mad Men* anticipated and stoked our fascination with the '60s—the show in many ways came to redefine our perception of the era.

A pattern-obsessed mind-set can help you spot opportunities in retro, nostalgia, economics, seasonality, and generational shifts. In just the last few years, we've seen the rebirth of many once red-hot products, such as Nike Air shoes, Schwinn cruiser bikes, and Moleskin classic notebooks.

Sometimes, entire industries are deeply rooted in cyclical patterns. Cyclicality is so fundamental to automotive design, for instance, that dozens of vehicles are specifically linked to old models. For example, in 1998, Volkswagen reintroduced its legendary Beatle with a curvy design reminiscent of the car's 1970s shape. Voted *Motor Trend* Car of the Year, the vehicle paved the way for other winning reincarnations, including the Mini Cooper and Fiat 500. Similarly, American muscle cars such as the Corvette, Camaro, and Mustang have spawned new cult followings and bridged generational gaps by maintaining retro design links.

Studying cyclical patterns in different industries is a way to cross-pollinate back to your own market. Retro-inspired car culture, for example, helped A&W spark a corporate turnaround. Launched in 1923, the company had been an undisputed leader until McDonald's started to dominate the fast-food market in the 1970s with its faster, cheaper burgers and a brightly colored design motif that appealed to children. A&W had been in a long, steady decline when it made a bold retro move in 1999. Revamping its look and feel to reconnect with its original drive-in audience—baby boomers—it reintroduced the original Burger Family product line along with Chubby Chicken and Root Beer Floats. Every point of customer contact touched on the '60s retro theme, turning A&W into one of fast food's biggest turnaround success stories.

But you don't have to dive too far into the past for cyclical opportunity. While retro cycles are based on generational recurrences, nostalgic cycles tap our collective memories. For example, over the last decade, Hollywood's blockbusters have dramatically shifted away from original screenplays to remakes of fairy tales, cartoons, and comics, including *Batman, Superman, X-Men, The Avengers, Snow White and the Huntsman, Alice in Wonderland,* and *Where the Wild Things Are*. Recently, I met Michael Lynton, Sony Entertainment's CEO, who explained another reason why nostalgic movies often win at the box office. They get a second wind from international markets, where consumers also grew up under the spell of the same fairy tales.

Economic cycles drive many opportunities, of course. Booms and busts make headline news, but companies typically fail to fully exploit these major shifts. During downturns, most companies become overly conservative, cutting back on inventory, R&D, and salaries. What they fail to see is that slack periods dramatically alter consumer spending habits, creating major opportunities for those nimble enough to adapt.

Take the case of Walmart. The company played it safe during

the recent downturn and delayed the building of new stores. But it also gambled by strategically upgrading existing stores, assuming that the gloomy economy would offer a chance to attract more middle-class customers seeking a superior discount retail experience. The result? Walmart's sales went from a nearly flat 1 percent growth in 2010 to 3.4 percent in 2011 and to 5.9 percent in 2012. In the same period, the company's stock rose more than 50 percent.

With an awareness of the constant nature of change and its resulting opportunity, you can be far better prepared for cyclical shifts. It takes a mind-set free of the stiff restraints of procedure and process to be able to leap obstacles like they don't exist.

DIAMOND LASHES AND A BILLION-DOLLAR VOICE

Born in 1928, Shu Uemura was the first man to graduate from the Tokyo Beauty Academy. In those days in Japan, men didn't become makeup artists, but Uemura grew up fascinated by cosmetics, art, and cinema. At twenty-seven, he crossed the Pacific to Hollywood, hoping to break into the motion picture makeup scene. He was anything but an instant hit. Seven years into his journey, thousands of miles from home, he failed to make a name for himself.

Then, one day in 1962, Uemura got his big break. The makeup artist for the Hollywood star Shirley MacLaine fell ill. Uemura, the stand-in, rose to the challenge, magically transforming the Caucasian starlet into a stunning Japanese icon for the hit movie *My Geisha*. Moviegoers were astounded by the superstar's transformation, and Uemura quickly became the most requested makeup artist in Hollywood. By 1964, he owned L.A.'s hottest makeup studio and had created his own school, ushering in ethnicity-mastering makeup techniques that remain in vogue today.

It would have been easy for Uemura to rest on his laurels, hobnobbing with the Hollywood elite. However, he couldn't help but realize that as America thrived, the rest of the world was economically in limbo and that the imbalance created a world enamored with American glamour. Uemura took that thinking to his home country, opening a second studio in Tokyo's trendiest district: Omotesandō. Over the next few decades, his global expansion would drive tens of millions in sales, leading to an acquisition by L'Oréal in 2004.

CAPITALIZING ON PERCEPTION

Over the next few years, global economies boomed, and by 2006, growing wealth was leading to a love of all things luxurious. Indeed, Trend Hunter was tracking bubbles of opportunity for glitzy products—such items as diamond-encrusted cakes, $20,000 martinis, $5,000 burgers, Swarovski crystal vodka bottles, and a half-million-dollar diamond-coated laptop. We called this "bling bling," and it came with a warning. When *mainstream* consumers are loving luxury, it's often a sign that a market is at its peak. For example, contrast this love of opulence with the darker mood in late 2011 when the Occupy Wall Street movement began and wealth-bashing the ultra-rich "one percent" was on the rise.

So how did Uemura capitalize on a luxury-loving mainstream market?

At the time, one of Uemura's celebrity clients was Madonna, who worked with Uemura's artistic director, Gina Brooke. One day, Brooke joked with the pop star, "Wouldn't it be amazing to have real, flawless diamonds on the lash line?" To Brooke's surprise, Madonna replied, "I love it! Can we do it tonight?"

When you're Madonna, you get what you want. Brooke quickly found a jeweler to cut the diamonds in time for Madonna's concert that night. She recalled, "We sat there on the floor and I glued about ten or twelve of them along each eye, and I was fanning them dry as she put her coat on."[1]

In just hours, Madonna and Brooke created the world's most expensive lashes—0.75 carats of glittering diamonds—in one of modern history's most fashionable examples of instant prototyping.

Some entrepreneurs would have been content with delighting their celebrity client. But Uemura saw a commercial opportunity. Before the media broke news of Madonna's sparkling lashes, Uemura stocked Neiman Marcus stores across America with the glittering accessory, selling the lashes for $10,000 per set. But the catch is that Uemura didn't expect to sell truckloads of diamond lashes: Uemura knew that even in boom times, the market for such a high-end product was limited. So just as Uemura's fame in both America and Tokyo capitalized on the *look* of another land, his company would capitalize on the *look* of Madonna's lashes. Uemura and his coworkers launched a faux version that sold for $25, making the glitter accessory available to all Madonna-mimicking teenage girls.

The budget-friendly fake luxury lashes pushed the company to an estimated $100 million in annual revenue, well before the market collapse. Just as Shu Uemura capitalized on the desire for glamor during the 1960s era of American prosperity, so he went on to capitalize on the desire for bling during a similar cycle of opulence in 2006.

What's intriguing is how these cyclical economic patterns created clusters of opportunity. Sometimes these opportunities come from a market in decline—as in the case of Walmart—and other times—as we saw with Uemura—from a market in peak. The key is to understand the economic context and plan accordingly.

Uemura's compelling story teaches us to step back and realize

---

1   Anastasia Hendrix, "Five Questions for Gina Brooke," *San Francisco Chronicle*, April 30, 2006, http://www.sfgate.com/living/article/FIVE-QUESTIONS-For -Gina-Brooke-Strike-a-pose-2498185.php.

that patterns repeat more often than people expect. You should always be paying attention to the forces influencing your business, such as economic cycles, and consider how these changes create new opportunities. But act fast, because the first to spot the opportunity tends to win biggest.

FROM "BLING BLING" TO BORING

As the saying goes, nothing lasts forever. By December of 2007, our research suggested that luxury was losing its luster. In March 2008, when the S&P 500 index was still a healthy 1,290, we published our first of three observations, titled "Bling Bling Boring." Over the next few months, our crowd-filtered algorithms revealed more patterns of frugality, which we termed "credit crunch couture," "rental culture," "small-budget gifting," "vintage retro," "do it yourself gifting," and "return to the kitchen."

We advised our clients to adopt a more conservative mind-set in advance of what seemed a likely financial collapse. I, too, battened down the hatches in my personal life. While I'd once owned a condominium, I was now happy to rent. I shifted to more conservative investments, and I refocused my life's research on how opportunity evolves in chaos. By October 2008, I'd finished my outline and chapter summaries for what was to become a timely book, *Exploiting Chaos: 150 Ways to Spark Innovation During Times of Change.*

By March 6, 2009, a year after we published "Bling Bling Boring," the S&P 500 had fallen 48 percent to 683. Lawrence Summers, the Director of the White House National Economic Council, reported that $50 trillion of global wealth had been erased, blaming an "abundance of greed and an absence of fear on Wall Street."[2]

---

2   Kevin Hechtkopf, "Summers: $50 Trillion in Global Wealth Has Been Erased," Associated Press, March 13, 1999, http://www.cbsnews.com/8301-503983_162 -4863891-503983.html.

Patterns such as "Bling Bling Boring" and "rental culture" had been canaries in the coal mine, warning of future economic distress. And as many of us painfully recall, the market did not bounce back for three long years!

When economies collapse, companies and individuals often find themselves paralyzed. But, as I've pointed out previously, during periods of intense change, cracks open that offer tremendous entrepreneurial opportunity.

Consider this partial list: Disney, CNN, MTV, Hyatt, Burger King, FedEx, Microsoft, Apple, Texas Instruments, 20th Century Fox, Gillette, AT&T, IBM, Merck, Hershey's, Eli Lilly, Coors, Bristol-Myers, Sun, Amgen, Autodesk, Adobe, HP, BMC, GE, Electronic Arts, and *Fortune* magazine. Each of these iconic firms was launched during an economic recession. During periods of turbulence, consumer needs quickly evolve, and if you're able to spot those shifting needs, you'll thrive.

With my finance background, I was curious to uncover potential upside bubbles associated with the collapse. At a high level, there was an obvious departure from the luxury of "bling" toward more frugal products. But there were many more offshoots that sprang from this shift. Here are some of the gems that popped up in 2007 and 2008:

RETURN TO THE KITCHEN It's natural to fear the worst when economic uncertainty strikes. Anticipate that people will buy more lima beans than steaks. But the situation was more complex in 2008. During downturns, people reevaluate their core values, and even for the wealthier, hardworking baby boomers, that meant a dramatic reconsideration of priorities. Boomers started placing a greater emphasis on life experience, family, and friends. In food, this meant a return to the kitchen: Cooking dinner was once again perceived as a time to bond with family. Many people assumed that this was just about saving money. It wasn't. There was a tremendous resurgence in the culinary arts, increased popularity of food shows, a proliferation of cooking blogs, growth online in food photography, increased interest in wine culture (which ironically is often expensive), and specialty products to elevate the home-cooked meal to modern foodie standards.

NEXT BESTING Stock market declines, job losses, and high unemployment naturally increase fears of financial risk. Even if you aren't struggling economically, you become more conscious of spending habits and avoid appearing ostentatious in front of neighbors who may be struggling. You might settle for a Toyota instead of a Lexus. Buy a $500 Calvin Klein suit or a $500 Kate Spade handbag instead of a $1,000 Hugo Boss suit or a $3,000 Prada purse. From home to business, you become more comfortable choosing the *next best* alternatives. This consumer mentality spawns opportunity for aggressive "next best" brands and companies to swing into action and steal customers from slower-moving competitors.

RENTAL CULTURE Desires don't disappear, even in the face of economic uncertainty. Empowered by the Internet, the Great Recession of 2008 sparked a rise in new businesses that streamlined the model of temporary ownership. Bag Borrow or Steal and Rent Me a Handbag created businesses out of renting designer purses that could be delivered directly to your door. Rent the Runway brought couture dresses from the runway to women across the globe. Zipcar, AutoShare, and Car2Go simplified car rentals, offering hourly renting. There's a hunting lesson here. Giant Hertz initially missed this opportunity, while rival Avis bought Zipcar for half a billion dollars in 2013.

NOSTALGIA MARKETING When gloom and doom prevail, we often seek refuge in rose-colored memories. This mind-set extends beyond marketing, with nostalgic brands such as Nintendo and Disney influencing runway fashion, and "storybook cinema" topping the box office.

CREDIT CRUNCH COUTURE Fashion moves like lightning—it's the lead indicator of major shifts in tastes, preferences, and styles. The 2008 economic downturn sparked a sharp rise in demand for vintage clothing, secondhand apparel, DIY attire, and smaller-scale, independent designers. Zara and H&M pioneered fast fashion, bringing high-fashion looks to the masses quickly and at reasonable prices. Empowered by this "credit crunch couture," Zara's Amancio Ortega saw his wealth skyrocket to an extraordinary $70 billion.

In retrospect, one might have predicted these clusters of opportunity. "Return to the kitchen" was not easy to anticipate based on past shifts in food consumption, but it was predictable if you thought about boomers and carefully observed the increased fascination with foodie culture. Before the Internet, rental culture was also not easy to imagine. But today, spurred by technologies developed specifically for the Internet, temporary ownership is a growing, alternative business model in a broad range of industries.

Whether you toil in a big company, own your business, or are an aspiring entrepreneur, it pays to develop a nose for cyclical patterns. Clearly, it pays to look into the past and think deeply and broadly about how vintage patterns might unfold in a modern context.

GETTING NASTY

Sophia Amoruso was a fashionable twenty-two-year-old who couldn't figure out what she wanted to do with her life. While living in her step-aunt's house, she dabbled with community college, but she couldn't stomach the idea of student debt. She knew she needed to find a way to make a living, and she hoped to identify a great opportunity in the process.

An avid user of the then-pioneering site MySpace, Amoruso had received a few messages from vintage clothing sellers on eBay who admired her sense of style. She wondered if an eBay store could be her calling. She scooped up a few choice items for $50 at her local Salvation Army and posted images to her new eBay shop. Women quickly showed appreciation for Amoruso's rare ability to curate styles from a bygone era. Her unique taste in vintage clothing epitomized retro, one-of-a-kind style, and her passion for photography helped attract attention. Amoruso had a great eye: One of her early finds was an $8 Chanel jacket that she quickly resold for $1,000. In a recent interview, Amoruso told me that the 100-fold markup convinced her of the opportunity. "It felt like winning the lottery."

Long before the days of hashtag campaigns and clothing line releases on Instagram, Amoruso used her social media skills to drive impressive traffic to her eBay store. She leveraged MySpace comments and feedback to study her customers, gauging reactions to clothing, models, and styles of imagery. She told me, "I posted bulletins and blog posts about every single auction, and I also responded to every comment that people would leave on my MySpace page."

Amoruso proceeded to develop new social media strategies to expand her fan following as she gained invaluable information about her customers' tastes and preferences and continued to curate an expanding range of unique pieces. Sales hit $115,000 in 2007, netting $20,000 in profit—enough for her to quit her day job and ditch her step-aunt's house for a place of her own.

A few rival eBay sellers attempted to sabotage her store by flagging it for innocuous reasons. "I think people were just pissed that my stuff was selling for so much," she said. "It was more about jealously than any particular thing that I was doing." The ordeal made her realize the limitations of online auctions: "eBay was a fantastic framework for launching a business, but it had a certain amount of impermanence to it," said Amoruso. "Your customers were eBay customers before they were yours, and you didn't have any way to communicate with them outside of eBay. I knew I was building a brand and that I wanted to own the experience end to end."

So, in June 2008, Amoruso launched NastyGal.com, a stand-alone online store (inspired by the 1975 Betty Davis album and the singer's style). Thanks in part to her impeccable taste and fashion savvy, and in part thanks to the fan base she had so meticulously built, NastyGal.com was an instant hit.

Up to this point, Amoruso's modest success was neatly anchored to the cyclical pattern of retro. But most retailers were unnerved by what seemed a much larger force: the economic downturn. In 2008, the American housing market and stock markets began to collapse, instantly shrinking consumer budgets and partly stigmatizing luxury items (the more bling you brandished, the less people thought of you). This ignited powerful trends that we've already discussed: "credit crunch couture," the drive toward vintage clothing, and "next besting," whereby consumers avoid the most expensive brands and look for alternatives.

Amoruso's timing was perfect: The financial markets were falling just as public interest in retro and vintage clothing was thriving. While other clothing retailers were cutting back to conservatively weather the economic storm, Amoruso thrived during the downturn. She ramped up her business, positioning NastyGal to become the vintage clothing market leader.

She filled a gap in the marketplace. San Francisco, L.A., and New York have dozens of trendy vintage shops in fashionable districts, but in most small towns, a shopper only finds vintage clothing in places such as the Salvation Army. Amoruso's well-photographed online shop provided a great alternative for thousands of credit-crunched, middle-class young women.

Over the next four years, economic uncertainty helped NastyGal become the fastest-growing retailer in America. Revenues soared from $115,000 in 2007, pre-recession, to an estimated $128 million in 2012, with an astonishing 60 percent gross margin.[3] That year *Forbes* placed Amoruso on its list of "ones to watch," estimating her net worth at $250 million.[4] Not bad for a twenty-nine-year-old who launched her empire from an eBay shop run from her aunt's basement.

Amoruso has since expanded beyond her initial vintage concept, offering fresh lines and styles that are similarly unique and reasonably priced. She's weathered setbacks, including a period in which she had to cancel 1,000 orders due to mix-ups and fulfillment issues. But for a business that grew 1,000-fold in five years, she's had pretty smooth sailing.

Amoruso teaches us that you can start small and grow quickly when you correctly identify and pursue a cyclical opportunity. Today's marketplace makes it easier than ever to prototype an idea and start selling, whether through an eBay store or a simple website. If your idea is unique and you've done your market research, you can carve out your small space and be in the right place at the right time when market cycles kick in.

THE REBIRTHING OF A BADASS BRAND

More than a century and a half ago, a long-bearded man named Hiram Walker made his first moonshine, and it was fantastic. He

3   Victoria Barret, "Nasty Gal's Sophia Amoruso: Fashion's New Phenom," *Forbes*, June 28, 2012, http://www.forbes.com/sites/victoriabarret/2012/06/28/nasty-gals-sophia-amoruso-fashions-new-phenom.

4   Nir Zuk, "Ones to Watch: Sophia Amoruso," *Forbes*, September 11, 2012, http://www.forbes.com/special-report/2012/forbes-400/ones-to-watch/profiles/0917_ones-to-watch_sophia-amoruso.html.

knew a whiskey venture could become his next big business, and in 1858, he built a distillery just over the border from Detroit in Windsor, Canada. Hiram Walker's Club Whiskey quickly took off. His was good whiskey—and even better branding. He'd added the word "club" to the name to play off the popular trend of imbibing in nineteenth-century gentlemen's clubs—the upscale, wood-paneled parlors of choice for men of distinction (not to be confused with today's neon-lit gentlemen's clubs that confer less distinction). Walker's "Club" branding paid off, becoming the top choice of patrons in both Canada and the United States.

The Canadian-based distillery was soon dominating its American competition, which responded by lobbying the U.S. government to force beverage brands to state their country of origin. But the defensive move backfired. In 1889, Walker's brilliantly rebranded Canadian Club Whisky acquired cachet as an imported luxury.

The Canadian Club factory was fueling so much trade that a company town, later named Walkerville, sprang up around the factory in 1890. Hiram Walker controlled it all, from police and fire department to religious services. He even built a church, but when the pastor spoke of the evils of alcohol, the church was abruptly closed. During the years of prohibition—long after Walker's death in 1899—his sons took the reins. Canadian Club's popularity exploded, becoming the contraband of choice for Al Capone, among others, who made millions smuggling the whiskey into the United States.

That advantage held for generations. Post-prohibition, Canadian Club was an American favorite for several decades, especially the 1960s when Canadian Club was still the whiskey of choice for New Yorkers who saw the logo shining down on Times Square. But like so many companies that reflect back on their glory days, the brand eventually lost its luster. Between its 1960s heyday and 2005, sales fell nearly 50 percent. In 2005, Canadian Club was acquired by Fortune Brands (later Beam Inc.), and a familiar strategy soon re-emerged: The company would spark renewal by reaching back into the whiskey's colorful and prosperous past.

Emerging from the shadows of an oak-walled boardroom, a mustachioed, macho father figure speaks to the camera. With glass in hand and a mischievous smile on his face, he strolls through a nineteenth-century mansion. "When America had this terrible idea called prohibition, Canada helped the U.S. out. Canadian Club was the most bootlegged whiskey in the states, and if there's one thing that tastes better than whiskey, it's smuggled whiskey." He explains, "I'm the Canadian Club Chairman. You're welcome." The catchy video is an advertisement, of course, and the fictional "Club Chairman," referred to by Jim Beam's branding committee as the "Badass Gentleman," soon became a potent symbol for the brand's playful, retro reincarnation.

Canadian Club's retro rebirth was also aided first by the popularity of *Mad Men,* in which suave ad exec Donald Draper seems to require his Canadian Club for fuel, and then by HBO's *Boardwalk Empire,* a drama that includes smuggling Canadian Club into the United States. The TV connections are dynamic. In one *Mad Men* episode, Draper grabs a bottle of Canadian Club, turns to his secretary, and growls, "Why is this empty?"

Mad Men didn't have a *formal* product placement relationship with the distillery, but as the show took off, the whiskey maker's marketing team doubled down on Canadian Club's vintage past. The objective: become the *other* drink for young men, when drinking beer doesn't cut it. One ad, often posted in men's urinals, showcased a cool, in-control ladies' man, kicking back in his wood-paneled, retro basement. There's a beautiful woman nestled in his lap and a glass of Canadian Club in his free hand. The provocative ad reads, "Your Mom Wasn't Your Dad's First." The ad said that your dad drank classy drinks—and nothing else. "He went out. He got two numbers in the same night. He drank cocktails. But they were whiskey cocktails." And the final line: "Damn right your dad drank it."[5] The ad tapped into retro by glamorizing the taboo imagery of this golden era. With clever advertising, retro 1960s style, and classic packaging, Canadian Club was deftly positioned as the drink of choice for those aspiring to capture old-world masculinity.

By reinvigorating its past, Canadian Club breathed new life into a declining brand. In 2012, sales of its CC's Reserve jumped 23 percent while sales of Sherry Cask doubled.[6] The point of all this: Most established companies can mine gold in their past. People are seduced by story, and if you can emphasize the right tales, you can cultivate a powerful connection to your brand.

The beauty of cyclical patterns is that they're predictable. You might cringe at your funky sweater from a decade ago, or that suit buried in the back of your closet that mocks your sense of style, but people all recognize that styles *repeat*. Many brands and entrepreneurs haphazardly clutch at these cycles, but others skillfully ride them like waves.

Another powerful takeaway is that to take advantage of a cyclical trend, you don't have to be first—you simply have to be fast-moving. Canadian Club wasn't the first to spot a retro opportunity. In fact, the company practically had the opportunity handed to it because *Mad Men*'s creators were placing the whiskey in the show organically. But when the opportunity surfaced, the company quickly reached out and grabbed it.

---

5   Canadian Club, "Canadian Club Whisky Looking for the Next Big Star for 'Damn Right Your Dad Drank It' Campaign: Could It Be You?," Marketwire.com, March 2009, http://www.marketwire.com/press-release/canadian-clubr-whisky -looking-next-big-star-damn-right-your-dad-drank-it-campaign-could-nyse-fo -1234739.htm.

6   Susan Krashinsky, "Canadian Club on the Rocks? Far From It, Thanks to Mad Men," *Globe and Mail*, April 19, 2012, http://www.theglobeandmail.com/report-on -business/industry-news/marketing/canadian-club-on-the-rocks-far-from-it-thanks -to-mad-men/article4105659.

EVERYTHING OLD IS NEW AGAIN

This chapter began with *Mad Men* and appropriately ends full cycle, much like the sea turtle, back where it began. *Mad Men* didn't just help Canadian Club shrug off its midlife crisis. The 1960s nostalgia that the show ushered into mainstream culture turned out to produce many opportunities for all kinds of companies and drinks. A bevy of carmakers eagerly advertised on the show, and the Gap's Banana Republic brand created a *Mad Men* collection in 2013 along with a series of promotions. In fact, the show's popularity sparked a frenzy of 1960s-related parties, products, and designs.

To conclude with some immortal television words, aptly uttered by *Mad Men*'s Donald Draper himself, "In Greek, 'nostalgia' literally means 'the pain from an old wound.' It's a twinge in your heart far more powerful than memory alone." Having delivered that observation, Draper continued in his baritone to pitch Kodak executives on the deeper appeal of their newfangled slideshow contraption, while slowly clicking through slides of his own family—back when they were happy. "This device isn't a spaceship, it's a time machine. It goes backwards, and forwards . . . It takes us to a place where we ache to go again. It's not called the wheel. It's called the carousel. It lets us travel the way a child travels—around and around, and back home again, to a place where we know we're loved." Such is the power of a cyclical trend.

SUB-PATTERNS OF CYCLICALITY

RETRO Digital photography has become ubiquitous, flooding our social streams with generic photos of everyday objects, friends, and events. To recall the artistic flair of days gone by, a team of twelve developers created Instagram, a social media app that artfully degrades your photos to match the vintage imperfection of early photography. Within two years, the team sold its business to Facebook for just over one billion dollars.

NOSTALGIA While the retro pattern brings back periods we might not have been a part of, nostalgia is about tapping our specific memories. *Toy Story* gave classic toys starring roles, successfully reincarnating several memorable brands from baby boomers' pasts, such as Mr. Potato Head, the Talking Chatter Phone, and the Etch A Sketch.

GENERATIONAL Old Spice deodorant once faltered because the brand failed to recognize that baby boomers don't perceive themselves as growing old. P&G was about to pull it from shelves before launching one last ad campaign starring macho Isaiah Mustafa as "The Man Your Man Could Smell Like." The ad, which targeted both the younger generation and boomers, was a huge hit. Attracting a phenomenal twenty million views, the ad (and numerous sequels) breathed new life into the brand, and sales quadrupled.

ECONOMIC In 1929, just three months after the stock market crashed, Henry Luce launched *Fortune* magazine. It was priced at the then-astronomical price of one dollar per issue, valuing the business publication the same as a wool sweater. Despite a pricey entry point, by the end of the 1930s, *Fortune* was attracting half a million subscribers and reaping $7 million per year in profit, an astounding feat for any expensive product during the Great Depression. At first, this seems counterintuitive, but Luce's genius was to realize that economic cycles create new, less-obvious needs. He was selling the long-term value of in-depth financial reporting—which was especially useful during a depression. Economic cycles always trigger new and often counterintuitive consumer needs, and in the 1930s, investors were hungry to understand corporate America—how it ended up in ruins, and how, where, and when it might reemerge.

SEASONAL Since the 1970s, retailers have gradually increased their operating hours on Black Friday, the day after Thanksgiving, which has become the biggest and most important day for retail sales. But it was not until 2011 that retailers elected to open when the clock struck midnight on Friday, a move led by Target, Best Buy, Kohl's, and Macy's. In retrospect, it's almost surprising it took retailers so long to exploit the opportunity. By the next year, Walmart had dramatically extended its Black Friday to start earlier in the week.

SUMMARY: CYCLICALITY

Throughout history, economic cycles have sparked patterns of opportunity. Just as we often fail to see the clear patterns in our own imperfect relationships and life choices, in times of boom and bust, we tend to see no further than the obvious, immediate trends. But as these economic cycles unfold, many larger patterns present themselves. Whiskey, bling, clothes, cars, bicycles, and food are just a few of the products that entrepreneurs and established companies have successfully reinvigorated by tapping into a cyclical pattern, borrowing imagery and story lines and profiting from people's memories and nostalgia.

TAKEAWAYS

1. **Expect Repetition** Many people fail to adapt to cyclical patterns, but if you expect repetition, you can open your mind to the clues that will lead to opportunity.

2. **Act Quickly** By definition, cyclical opportunities are fleeting. To win, you'll need to move fast when you sense an opening, just as Shu Uemura's designer prototyped diamond lashes in a single day and the company then turned a publicity stunt into a hit product.

3. **Anticipate the Certainty of Evolution** It's easy to get swept up in current, well-planned scenarios and the comfort of the status quo, but preparing for what's next can produce an asymmetric advantage.

4. **Look Beyond What Others Already See** We tend to see what's immediate, such as the collapse or surge of prices in a stock market. But major forces create cascading effects. As an economic cycle unfolds, many smaller opportunities gradually present themselves. You need to go where the opportunity will be next, not where it is. Like Sophia Amoruso digging through a Salvation Army bin of dusty clothes and coming away with a classic Chanel jacket, you must be on the hunt for the most subtle of opportunities.

Chapter 8

REDIRECTION

REDIRECTION: The art of channeling the power of a trend, behavior, or demonstration of need instead of fighting it. Includes: refocusing, reprioritizing, rationalizing, reversing, and gamifying.

Redirection involves skillfully reframing a product, service, or issue to your advantage. Think of Avis turning the pain of being the long-suffering number two rent-a-car company into one of the most successful redirect taglines in advertising history: "We try harder (when you're not the biggest, you have to)."

Politicians have long practiced subtle redirection in the form of "spin," taking a controversy and channeling it in a direction more helpful to their campaign. More recently, Volkswagen launched a competition called The Fun Theory, challenging contestants to solve everyday problems using "fun" concepts that reframe convention. A favorite example was an entry by Kevin Richardson aimed at changing our driving habits.

Consider speeding and our perception of the police. While in principle cops are devoted to serving and protecting the people in their community, that's rarely how most of us view law enforcement. Many drivers, for instance, have a strong adversarial view of police cars for a simple reason. We worry that each cop car we spot is out to ticket us for something. This creates an awkward dynamic in which we often perceive law enforcement as a foe.

Richardson's solution was called "The Speed Camera Lottery."

Cameras were installed on a busy Stockholm street, and over three days, they took snapshots of 24,857 cars. Richardson explained, "A camera photographs speeders and gives them a citation, and that money goes into a pot. But if you're obeying the law your picture will be snapped, and you'll be entered into a lottery and win some of that money from speeders."[1] The result was a 22 percent reduction in speeding.

In another experiment for The Fun Theory, people were encouraged to take the stairs rather than the escalator. Music and playfulness was the redirect. They turned the stairs into a virtual piano (à la Tom Hanks in the movie *Big*) and generated a phenomenal change in behavior. The trickle of stair walking promptly turned into a flood. Young and old danced up, down, and around the stairs in spontaneous, often joyful celebrations that generated a stunning 66 percent increase in stair walking.

Next, the same group did an experiment to reduce littering. Most countries issue citations for littering that rarely help reduce the problem. In Stockholm, researchers wanted to see if they could get more people to throw rubbish in trash bins by making it fun. To this end, they installed a device with recorded random sound effects at the bottom of a public trash bin. Imagine hurriedly passing a garbage can, tossing in a random piece of trash, and being met with the zips, zooms, squeaks, and squeals you'd expect from a video game. Moms with babies and children began gathering around the magical bin, throwing in whatever trash they could find. In a single day, 72 kilos of trash were dropped in the bin—41 kilos more than normal.

What these experiments demonstrate is how many routines or

---

1   Kevin Richardson, "The Speed Camera Lottery," The Fun Theory, November 12, 2010, http://www.thefuntheory.com/speed-camera-lottery-0.

traditional situations can be redirected through a novel approach. The biggest step is to acknowledge that the old ways won't cut it. You can't fight an unstoppable force, but you can channel momentum to your advantage.

PEEING CONTESTS, BEER, AND THE POWER OF A CLEVER REDIRECT

How do you stop men from committing a more noxious form of littering—urinating on the city streets? That task may seem beyond the realm of a business book, but as it turned out, Waternet, Amsterdam's water utility, found the solution to this real dilemma in the power of the redirect.

Every year, to mark the Queen's birthday, the Dutch don their beloved orange attire and celebrate in the streets with twenty-four hours of public drinking. It's Mardi Gras for the Dutch, except the streets get flooded with much more than patriotism: it's a veritable yellow tide. Throughout the celebrations, men unabashedly relieve themselves in the streets and canals. They call it *pissen gehen*, and you don't have to speak Dutch to know what that means. A Waternet official explained, "A lot of people can't tell the difference between a toilet and a canal on Queen's Day."[2]

So put yourself in the position of Waternet. To them, the drunken streams were not just disgusting, but a real threat to the environment and to public health. The utility estimated that on each Queen's Day, 11,500 liters (3,000 gallons) of urine spilled into the canals. And it gets worse. The canals are also the source of the city's drinking water.

So how to redirect "the flow"? With one million people partying

---

2 "ACHTUNG! for Waternet on Queensday 2012 Advertising Campaign," May 9, 2012, http://youtu.be/wvOh6fvIQPc.

throughout the city, misbehavior becomes unstoppable. Fines would only provoke dissent. *Pissen gehen* had become a countercultural celebration rite.

Instead of ordering the end of *pissen gehen,* Waternet *redirected* behavior. The utility accepted the reality that drunken celebrants get rebellious. Instead of fighting the trend, they dreamed up ways to channel rebellion's momentum. Enlisting Achtung, a digital ad agency, Waternet developed Potje Pissen, an interactive, video-game-like urinal system. Potje Pissen was a new kind of outdoor competitive game not unlike carnival water pistol games. Without the pistol. All you needed was a full bladder and good aim to win.

The clever name means "piss off." Achtung's promotional video half-jokingly suggested, "To get [men] peeing in the right spot, we created a toilet system that rewards every drop."[3]

People quickly got into the spirit, eager to outdo their friends (some women even joined in). Waternet even offered to pay the annual utility bill for the city's Grand Champion Pisser. When you think about the target market—young intoxicated males—it's easy to understand how the game took off. Waternet spun misbehavior into diligence by turning it into a fun contest.

The game was a triumph. It protected the canal by deftly shifting public behavior, and it changed the perception of the utility to one that embraced fun and creativity. By not taking itself too seriously, Waternet seemed more relatable and fun. That connection has enabled the utility to more successfully broadcast its underlying message, generating a longer-term redirection of public misbehavior. Far from fighting the mischievous tradition, Waternet made it even *more fun,* while achieving its own ends in the process.

This challenge may sound unusual, but it was important. Dealing with a massive, unruly crowd cried out for a shift in thinking,

---

3   "Achtung! for Waternet on Queensday 2012," Promotional Video, https://www
.youtube.com/watch?v=5_Dmuf1Mtuw.

which is part of the magic of redirection. Ultimately, the lesson is that you can't fight an unstoppable force, but you can channel momentum to your advantage.

ROYAL POTATOES, PINK SLUDGE, AND ESCAPING A BASHTAG

Frederick II was a relentlessly creative innovator who dreamed of making a difference. Music and culture were his first passions, but his father demanded focus on the family trade. Freddy resisted and ran away, but he was captured, returned home, and forced into the family business. Freddy's first lesson was that you can't get far from home when your dad is the King of Prussia.

Later named Frederick the Great for his military prowess, Freddy eventually took over for his dad. An early trend spotter, Freddy scoured the world in pursuit of innovation, eloquently noting, "The greatest and noblest pleasure which we have in this world is to discover new truths, and the next is to shake off old prejudices."[4] One idea that caught his eye was a miracle food from South America: the potato. Freddy saw potential in Prussian potatoes, and he introduced the crop to his people. But he couldn't convince many that the potato—brown, lumpy, and hard—was worth eating.

Freddy tried a different tactic: He made potatoes compulsory. Yes, it became law that all citizens must eat potatoes. But when he issued an order in 1774 for his subjects to grow potatoes as protection against famine, the people of Kolberg replied, "The things have neither smell nor taste, not even the dogs will eat them, so what use are they to us?"[5] Like children being told to eat vegetables, they resisted the dull, mandated taste of potatoes.

---

4 *Orissa Review*, Home Department, Government of Orissa, 1890.

5 *Discovery: A Monthly Journal of Popular Knowledge* (1949): 311.

Finally, Freddy publicly gave up. He declared that potatoes were now royal vegetables, to be eaten only by royals. His precious potatoes were now off-limits. Henceforth, they would be planted only in the royal garden, and guarded—albeit in a calculatedly lackluster way.

Of course, Freddy knew that by doing this he'd trigger a desire for the forbidden food. Not unlike Red Bull's strategy of putting warnings on their labels, the king was employing a clever bit of reverse psychology. Soon it seemed that nearly everyone was stealing, planting, and eating Prussian potatoes. Yet, mysteriously, not one person was punished. The king ultimately got his wish—potatoes became a hit. The point: By understanding the rebellious mind-set of his subjects, Freddy revolutionized the Prussian food chain.

Fast-forward 300 years, and Freddy's potatoes are now a staple at McDonald's. But the loved and loathed restaurant giant is subject to similar criticism and damaging rumors from patrons who ask, "Have you ever wondered why McDonald's fries never rot?" or "How do they turn pink sludge into chicken McNuggets?" or "Is it really beef, or just a trademarked brand called '100% Pure Beef'?"

Confronting rumors has become essential to brands in our social media–fueled age. Like Frederick the Great, it was useless for McDonald's to try to stem the tide of public comments about their food quality; instead, they needed to ride that momentum by broadcasting the benefits of the chain's food in an unconventional way. In 2012, the company seized the microphone, sponsoring a huge #McDStories Twitter campaign in the hope that customers would share fun and nostalgic McDonald's memories, which would, in turn, promote the brand. Alas, the results weren't what the company expected.

Within an hour, thousands were broadcasting McDonald's-shaming stories: "I ate a McFish and vomited 1 hour later"; "Fingernail in my BigMac"; "I could smell Type 2 diabetes floating in the air and I threw up." Traditional media added fuel to the fire. The most unflattering tweets were now generating millions of negative impressions in dozens of newspapers. *Forbes* magazine summed up the disaster in an article titled, "From Hashtag to Bashtag."

As Frederick the Great and McDonald's both learned, there's a big difference between inauthentic messaging of a product and knowing the subtle steps to shift perceptions. McDonald's recognized the megatrend of social media, but failed to appreciate the convergence of several competing trends, such as brand-bashing and the need for corporate authenticity.

Undaunted by its initial flop, McDonald's returned with "Your Questions Answered," a campaign dreamed up by an intern that had just the right mix of transparency and humility. In video and text, McDonald's managers pledged to respond to "any question that doesn't have profanity."

Many customers asked a question I'd often wondered about: "Why do the burgers never look the same as they do in the photos?" The marketing director delivered the first YouTube video response. She recorded herself purchasing an actual burger and working through all of the preparation steps that lead to a billboard-ready burger. Surprisingly honest, the video generated 8 million impressions, positive reviews, more loyalty for the brand, and a whole series of surprisingly authentic and successful inside looks at the people and food of McDonald's.

Social media has created a new playing field, making spin and psychology far more important tools than before. When your product comes face-to-face with adversity or rumors, careful, redirected communication can put the conversation in a much more positive light.

The potential for a product or an idea to go viral changes the payoff curve. If McDonald's had simply answered each question privately, the company might have changed a few minds, but it would have done little to change its overall perception. But by producing deep, thoughtful videos, showing the faces and personalities of the men and women behind the scenes, the company created shareable entertainment that triggered millions of views and shifted public opinion about its products.

MANUFACTURING DESIRE

You have the power to reposition reality.

For more than half a century, we've been mesmerized by the priceless perception of diamond rings, spending literally tens of billions of dollars on sparkling rocks. But from a financial perspective, store-bought diamond jewelry lacks intrinsic, investable value. Diamond jewelry is similar to wine triple-marked-up in a restaurant. Once a ring buyer exits the store, his or her shiny new purchase loses as much as 65 percent of its value. Even more surprising, diamonds haven't always been a girl's best friend. Before 1938, the ritual of exchanging engagement rings was by no means pervasive, and the stones themselves were not considered rare.

Today, the diamond industry is flourishing, with many players selling niche divergent products such as conflict-free diamonds and laser-engraved diamonds. My curiosity about the industry was sparked a couple of years ago when I delivered a keynote to those in the trade. Several conversations with dealers and executives had me diving deep into the history of America's favorite rock.

Interestingly, unlike precious metals, which can be melted down and sold for their intrinsic value, diamonds are simply an extreme form of carbon, the most ubiquitous element in the universe. Authentic, certified diamonds can be fabricated using intense pressure or explosive detonation. They can also be grown using a laboratory process called chemical vapor deposition, or CVD. This intricate process layers a diamond with such precision that the resulting rocks are structurally superior to mined diamonds.

So if diamonds were never truly rare, and today you can fabricate more-perfect versions of them in a lab, how did they become the marker of true love? The answer is a dark lesson in the power of launching a novel trend. The manufactured desire for diamonds is perhaps one of history's most famous examples of a company exploiting a redirection pattern.

Our tale begins in the 1870s. Funded by British financiers, diamond mines in Brazil and India were yielding modest quantities of the semiprecious gem. But over the next few decades, massive South African deposits were discovered. To stop these diamonds from flooding the world market, the British organized a cartel called the De Beers Consolidated Mines, Ltd. By controlling all distribution, stockpiling diamonds, and regulating supply, the cartel kept diamonds scarce and prices high. But this financial achievement came at a high human cost. Mired in controversy, De Beers has been soundly criticized for exploiting African laborers and nations and for masterminding an international monopoly that manipulated supply and prices.

In the early twentieth century, diamond engagement rings were uncommon, and American demand for diamonds was plummeting. By 1919, demand was down 50 percent from its peak a few decades earlier. Wealthy buyers pursued other precious stones and metals, such as rubies, sapphires, and gold. In 1938, De Beers brought that problem to N.W. Ayer & Son, a top New York–based advertising agency. The goal was to invent a deep emotional association between diamonds and romance. In 1981, memos from Ayers to De Beers were uncovered by *The Atlantic*, which paraphrased the strategy: "It would be crucial to inculcate in [young men] the idea that diamonds were a gift of love: the larger and finer the diamond, the greater the expression of love."[6]

To make this happen, De Beers would need to create a strong

---

6   Edward Jay Epstein, "Have You Ever Tried to Sell a Diamond," *The Atlantic*, February 1982, http://www.theatlantic.com/past/issues/82feb/8202diamond1.htm.

perception that affluent people want diamonds and that they're so valuable that women will never part with them.

The De Beers redirection program began in earnest with an elaborate, multitiered plan to tie diamonds to wedding proposals, modern civilization's ultimate symbol of youthful love and, less glamorously, its promise of financial stability. Over the next year, De Beers facilitated and broadcasted movie stars, British royalty, and celebrities giving diamonds as gifts of love. Diamonds were product placed in motion pictures, and public relations campaigns resulted in designers and celebrities talking about the trend toward diamonds. Given its British ties, De Beers was even able to arrange highly publicized visits by the Queen to South African diamond mines. One of the first celebrity rags, *Hollywood Personalities,* paid particular attention to diamond rings. Full-color ads, rare and expensive at the time, were featured with historic works of art placed next to diamonds.

By 1947, sales had grown significantly, but N.W. Ayer & Son still felt that the psychological link needed to be strengthened. "We are dealing with a problem in mass psychology," a memo noted. "We seek to . . . strengthen the tradition of the diamond engagement ring—to make it a psychological necessity capable of competing successfully at the retail level with utility goods and services."[7]

In executing this strategy, a copywriter named Frances Gerety dreamed up the phrase "A diamond is forever," the jewel in a multi-million-dollar national campaign that today remains the hallmark of De Beers. Despite the deeply troubling aspects of international diamond production, the slogan would help make the diamond ring an enduring societal expectation. A few years later, the diamond's iconic status was strengthened in the 1949 Broadway show *Gentlemen Prefer Blondes,* in which Carol Channing purred, "Diamonds are a girl's best friend." By the time the film version, starring

---

7   Ibid.

Marilyn Monroe, rolled out in 1953, diamonds had become the ultimate declaration of romance. In 2000, *Advertising Age* named "A diamond is forever" the best advertising slogan of the twentieth century.

Positioning the diamond engagement ring as an iconic expression of love was a tremendously profitable redirection. By associating its product with commitment and engagement, De Beers created a virtually unbreakable psychological link. The De Beers story is also a unique tale of how companies craft perceptions. De Beers was able to redirect millions of people around the world into believing that diamonds were rare and necessary for love, while directing attention away from the massive human suffering required to mine them. It's a cautionary tale, but also proof of the power of redirection.

One of the most significant redirection takeaways from De Beers is the value of carefully associating your product with something greater—whether it be a positive action, ritual, tradition, or emotion. By consistently reinforcing this link, your product can draw on cultural forces to propel it to success. For example, Coca-Cola benefits from a strong link to the emotion of happiness, which is carefully messaged in all of its ad campaigns through jingles, singing, and holiday marketing. Apple, meanwhile, is strongly linked to music and simplicity.

In a more entrepreneurial example, consider the story of what happened when Carol Aebersold, a writer, and her twin daughters Chanda Bell and Christa Pitts, wrote a book called *The Elf on the Shelf: A Christmas Tradition*. It's a charming family story about an elf who travels each night (to let Santa know who's been naughty and nice) and magically appears somewhere new in your home the next morning. "You could find him anywhere, from your freezer (which reminds him of the North Pole) to hanging from your chandelier," wrote *FOX Business*. "Children are told not to touch the elf, as he will lose his magic, but they're encouraged to tell him any special messages they have for Santa."[8] Every major publisher rejected the children's story with such choice put-downs as "children don't like rhyming books" and "this is destined for the damaged goods bin" and, Pitts's personal favorite, "maybe someone else should write it." But the family wouldn't be deterred. They self-published, and they threw an elf doll in with the package.

By explicitly positioning *Elf on the Shelf* as a wonderfully playful tradition, the elf and book became linked to the holiday, resulting in a colossal success. In 2011 alone, sales topped $16 million.

SUB-PATTERNS OF REDIRECTION

RATIONALIZING If your product has a feature or an attribute that stands out, you can use justification to turn an oddity into the core benefit. I grew up listening to Buckley's popular cough syrup slogan, "It's awful and it works!" This was a clever redirect that turned the syrup's sour taste into a proof point. Similarly, Volvo cars were long seen as unattractive, but then the company drew attention to their safety and increased sales with the famous campaign "They're boxy but they're good." Finally, digital-based financial institutions ranging from eTrade to ING spun their lack of physical branches as—rather than an inconvenience—savings for customers.

REFOCUSING Karen Klein is a sixty-eight-year-old former school bus driver who was bullied and victimized by a bus full of horrible kids. Incredibly, they even had the gall to video their verbal abuse and upload it to YouTube. Most of the millions of people who watched the footage were disgusted. One viewer in particular, named Max Sidorov, created an Indiegogo crowd-funding campaign to treat

---

8   Michele Heilies, "Are You Sitting on Your 'Elf on the Shelf'?," *FOX Business*, December 20, 2012, http://smallbusiness.foxbusiness.com/entrepreneurs/2012/12/20/are-sitting-on-your-elf-on-shelf.

Karen to a vacation. More than $650,000 was donated to the campaign in less than a week, and it was given to Klein (she then launched the Karen Klein Anti-Bullying Foundation). Sidorov flipped the focus of the viral attention from bullying and derision and refocused the conversation on a nobler cause.

REPRIORITIZING Sometimes it pays to deprioritize perfection. Theo Lioutas, one of my clients, discovered this when he was the director of new products and technology at Tropicana. The juice maker's early success was tied to its premium quality and certification as a Florida Grade A orange juice. Lioutas explained that the grading meant the juice was flawless according to rigid guidelines, including pulp-free purity. The single-minded pursuit of this rating, however, began to suppress internal innovation because nobody dared introduce products that might jeopardize the seal. By shifting focus away from the "Grade A" branding, the company was able to liberate creativity and eventually develop Homestyle juice, effectively becoming the first mass-produced juice with pulp and helping Tropicana develop into the world's largest juice maker.

REVERSING Teddy Roosevelt was set to launch a nationwide campaign tour when his team realized it had printed a million flyers without permission to use a copyrighted photo. What's more, the photographer normally demanded $1 for each use of the image. Without time to reprint new flyers, Roosevelt personally approached the photographer. Instead of asking for a quote, he reversed his approach and explained that he was thinking of using the photo, which with the accompanying photo credit would bring the artist tremendous publicity. Roosevelt offered the artist the right for a hundred dollars, and yes, the artist paid up.

SURPRISING An unexpected surprise can go a long way, especially with respect to products or services for which consumers have built-in expectations. Air travel, for example, is an industry that consumers generally perceive as a necessary evil. People often assume that few airlines truly care about their customers. To redirect people's focus from all the reasons to detest air travel, KLM airlines sought out passengers with social media profiles, figured out their likes, and then surprised them with gifts in their seats. Similarly, WestJet airlines placed a digital message to Santa for passengers checking in for a flight. Kids and adults alike scanned their boarding pass and told Santa what they wanted for Christmas. By the time the passengers landed, the airline had scrambled to surprise everyone with their desired gift. The video of the Santa flight racked up 20 million views in its first week.

GAMIFYING For years, we've seen the power of reward programs in travel, credit card usage, and even fast-food restaurants. Over the last few years, there has been significant progress in researching gaming mechanisms and applying that theory to real-world problems, as we saw from the story of Waternet, Amsterdam's water utility. SPARX is another example of a gaming mechanism. It's a new game that helps kids handle depression by teaching them how to master difficult situations (SPARX won the United Nations World Summit Award). Kahnoodle is an app that helps couples by giving each person challenges (and rewards) for spicing up their relationship. And Sleepcycle is a phone app that tracks your sleeping habits, including how often you move around in your bed, snore, and so on. The next wave consists of non–gaming companies that are building gamification into their workforce, products, and sales strategies. OTower, for example, has worked with utility companies to gamify power savings for households by introducing neighborhood power comparisons. The company's gaming efforts saved two terawatts of energy in 2013, nearly enough to power Las Vegas for a year. By distracting people from the fact that what they are doing is "work," companies can motivate employees and customers to be more efficient and productive and have fun in the process.

SUMMARY: REDIRECTION

Instead of competing against a force or rebelling against it, redirection involves refocusing, shifting, swapping, repurposing, repositioning, righting a wrong, and gamifying an experience. It's the art of the spin. Far from just being about a politician's message, redirection can be a powerful tool for a hunter.

TAKEAWAYS

1. **Don't Fight a Force If You Can Rechannel It** With redirection, you aren't following a trend or opposing it. You're shifting focus to your advantage and then capitalizing on the momentum. It can be an easier, more effective tool for navigating bad PR or other difficult situations.

2. **Gamify Intended Behavior** If your challenge requires a shift in human behavior, consider the effectiveness of gaming. People love to play and are already familiar with dozens of gaming models and scenarios. Gamifying is a convenient and effective shortcut to redirection.

3. **Master the Art of Spin** Politicians have long used subtle forms of redirection under the label "spin," taking a controversy or a public outcry and channeling it in a direction more helpful to their campaign. Companies and entrepreneurs have the same opportunity, but often they miss out because, at first glance, the counterintuitive approach is more difficult to spot.

4. **Don't Blindly Chase the First "Big" Trend** Both Frederick the Great and McDonald's found a big idea they were eager to exploit, but like so many others, in their initial effort, they blindly raced into new terrain without considering the potential outcomes. Better to watch and wait before pouncing.

5. **Engineer Success Through Psychology** Burned by early blunders, both King Frederick and McDonald's tried other strategies. Frederick used reverse psychology to tempt his subjects into trying something new. Meanwhile, McDonald's shrewdly dealt with negative rumors by handling them in a controlled, video environment in which it was easier to shape the dialogue.

Chapter 9

REDUCTION

REDUCTION: Simplifying a business concept or focusing it more on a specific idea. Includes: specialization, removing layers and steps, fractioning, crowd-sourcing, subscriptions, localization, and efficiency.

Bigger is better, or so we're trained to believe. Unfortunately, this quest for size misguides us and causes people to miss the little concepts that might mushroom into thriving opportunities. Single-purpose shops for cupcakes, yogurt, fresh juice, or grilled cheese sandwiches are all examples of thriving, real-world businesses that capitalize on small-batch specialization.

Online, new niche breakout successes are birthed every week, such as Dollar Shave Club, which keeps lazy men on top of their grooming products with monthly deliveries, or Just White Shirts, a multimillion-dollar business for guys with simple tastes.

Meanwhile, broadcasting has shifted toward hyper-niche reality shows, such as *House Hunters, Toddlers and Tiaras, Ice Truckers,* and *Pawn Stars.* Trend Hunter even helped capitalize on this trend five years ago, crowd-sourcing niche game-show ideas for billionaire Jon de Mol, creator of *Fear Factor* and *Big Brother.*

Reductive opportunities are sometimes overlooked, because going after smaller and simpler markets often means you have to "give something up." Business owners tend to worry about the trade-off without realizing that consumers actually prefer products that are specific to narrowly defined needs.

In consumer electronics, for example, cameras, phones, laptops, and tablets initially evolved through adding features, speed, and power. But the highest-grossing digital-imaging brand in December of 2012 wasn't Canon or Nikon, but the new kid on the block, GoPro—makers of a simple, wide-angle video camera optimized for action experiences. The uncomplicated camera has just two buttons: one for power and another for options. There is no standard viewfinder and there are no lens options. Just point and shoot. At $300 to $400, the GoPro isn't cheap, but neither is it outrageous. Many customers buy multiple GoPros to capture their adventures from different angles (I own four: two for work, two for fun).

When adventure enthusiast Nicholas Woodman founded GoPro back in 2003, the photography industry was dominated by giants such as Kodak, Canon, and Nikon. Despite their broad range of products, none of these giants had a simple camera to suit Woodman's needs when he wanted to immortalize his surfing conquests. Smartphones, digital SLRs, and multifunction cameras were too cumbersome to capture his exploits. So Woodman strapped a Kodak disposable camera to his wrist and took to the waves. With each additional prototype, he made something simpler. A year later, he had a basic camera whose sales would help him become a billionaire in less than a decade.

Most people understand the power of niche products and demographic segments. But that doesn't always lead to action. Misguidedly, many CEOs pursue the mass market when it would have been smarter to think smaller. This wrongheaded approach frequently happens in big companies, and the result is a watered-down value proposition that simply can't inspire brand love. If you want people to love what you stand for, you need to create products that are irresistible to a specific group.

Reduction is about the power of niche and simplicity at its extreme. It's about products and services so targeted that they sparkle amid the clutter of an everything-to-everyone world.

Let's begin with a simple idea born from one of the worst emotional pains a person can imagine.

DIAMONDS, RED WINE, AND BROKEN HEARTS

Sometimes opportunity lurks in an individual's greatest failures.

Josh Opperman was a New York City market researcher who had it all figured out. Then, after a busy day working for *Wine Spectator* magazine, he returned home to his Manhattan apartment to find his fiancée gone. After years of courtship and three months of seemingly blissful engagement, she'd left only one artifact behind: the $10,000 engagement ring he'd given her. He explains, "The beautiful diamond engagement ring was sitting on the coffee table looking up at me as if to say, 'So, what's next?'"[1]

Devastated, Opperman cleared out the apartment and set out to return the ring. At least he could get back his money. Or so he thought. It turned out that the jeweler wasn't willing to buy it back at anywhere near full price. As with almost all diamond engagement rings, the jeweler's wholesale cost was about a third of retail. Opperman's $10,000 diamond ring was only worth about $3,500. Now Opperman was feeling not only dumped, but financially duped.

Although tempted to take the cash and move on, he decided to see if he could create a better option. He learned that precious metals, such as gold and silver, have an intrinsic value that makes your granny's gold necklace worth more today than in days gone by. Diamond rings are different, and as he broadened his research, he uncovered a unique opportunity.

---

1   Josh Opperman, "Our Founder's Story," I Do Now I Don't, accessed September 1, 2014, https://www.idonowidont.com/I-do-founder-josh-opperman-story.

What does a heartbroken guy do when he needs to unload an expensive ring? Pawnshops, eBay, and Craigslist are options, but each has drawbacks. "I read so many complaints about people getting scammed on eBay," Opperman told me. "People are selling fake pieces, cubic zirconia [stones as diamonds], fake Tiffany settings."

In 2007, Opperman and his sister launched a web business called I Do Now I Don't. The site was launched with just a few thousand dollars, and Opperman viewed it as no more than a little side project. But his sister was a talented public relations professional. She began writing press releases, and three weeks later, Opperman was appearing on CNN.

Depressing as it may sound, I Do Now I Don't snowballed into the largest outlet for heartbroken young men and women wanting to rid themselves of unwanted engagement rings. Bargain hunters save by paying far less than retail, and sellers recover, on average, more than half of what they spent. The extra pain point Opperman solved was the need for safe transactions, verified by a gemologist. By removing this hurdle, he created a multimillion-dollar market for safe jewelry sales.

Within a few years, Opperman was brokering the sale of more than a thousand rings a year, with price points ranging from $1,000 to $30,000. In 2012, that added up to over $3 million in revenue. His business has even begun to attract competitors—always the sign of success—such as DivorceYourDiamond.com and Exboy friendJewelry.com.

Given that there are roughly 1 million breakups per year in the United States alone, Opperman estimates that the potential U.S. market for his business is 1.7 million wedding rings annually, totaling $4.2 billion in retail pricing. (And if that's not a rosy enough ending to his recent heartbreak, along the way he found the real love of his life and is now happily married.)

When I interviewed Opperman, he was clear about the value of simplification. "If you focus on one idea at first, and you do it right, you can be more successful," he said. "If we had sold all types of jewelry, it would have been a lot more difficult."

The niche focus of his business creates a marketing advantage, but that's not all; there's a further reductive pattern in his business model. Opperman simplifies the transaction by reducing the number of layers between buyer and seller. In a related example, I interviewed Vashi Dominguez, a European who used to wholesale diamonds until he decided to start his own website for direct sales. He explained, "I used to deal with the mines and the factory, but when I saw the huge markups in the retail world, I saw opportunity. There were five layers! What a great opportunity to cut out the clutter." Within seven years, he grew his online jewelry business, Vashi .com, to $25 million in sales.

Opperman also recognizes that part of his success was in turning lemons into lemonade. "The best businesses are trying to solve real-world problems," he told me. "Usually your best ideas come from personal experiences. You try something but get frustrated because you can't find anything like it." If you've been disappointed by a product or business, Opperman's story suggests that you should act on that frustration. Millions of other potential customers may be experiencing similar frustrations. The Internet enables entrepreneurs to take these niche ideas and turn them into profitable ventures.

Sometimes the simplest and smallest ideas take off. You'll see this illustrated in our next story, which involves a concept that began with what you might call a five-dollar idea.

WHAT WILL *YOU* DO FOR FIVE BUCKS?

You don't need a *big* idea if it's possible to take a *little* idea and make it big.

What can you get for five bucks? More than you might imagine.

Trend Hunter once paid five bucks to a Steve Irwin impersonator to jump out of the jungle in a video warning about the most dangerous species of wild animal in the entire kingdom: "The Trend Hunter." In total, Trend Hunter paid just $1,000 to get 200 people around the world to do little—but clever—things to market our business.

These five-buck conquests were made possible by a site called Fiverr, the world's largest marketplace for micro-tasks. Thousands of people offer their unique services on the site for a fee. And while the gigs might start at $5, many sellers offer extras that raise their fees, making the site a profitable source of income. And the Fiverr experience is just as beneficial to those seeking services. Let's say, for example, you're launching a new business. Fiverr has people who can design your business cards, edit your letters, animate your logo, craft a short commercial video, record a jingle, or translate your brochure. The site also makes available business tips, legal work, branding, and financial consulting. You can even get help with your elevator pitch.

Micha Kaufman and Shai Wininger founded the company in 2009 with the goal of removing the hurdles to hiring or freelancing. Experienced entrepreneurs, they knew firsthand how tricky it can be to hire experts for short-term work. "There is pain in that process," Kaufman told me. "There was a very focused idea to be destructive and simple. We started thinking about where the idea could lead."

Their key observation was how much time is wasted finding people and negotiating contracts. That barrier has prevented many experts from offering simple, low-cost services. Kaufman explained, "There has been this amazing explosion of super-talented people with some kind of skill that someone else on the other end of the globe might need. Imagine what could happen if you could connect the talent with the need."

Kaufman knew he "needed to be very simple. We needed a starting point to get to the minimum ingredients for people to get interested. So, for example, we wanted everything on Fiverr to work in no more than five minutes. To buy something should not take more than twenty to thirty seconds. And price negotiation is a huge friction, so it needed to be removed. We made just one price, which was to be the price of a cappuccino. We wanted something so simple that no matter what you might get back, you would never be upset."

Three years post-launch, Fiverr now lists more than 2 million services, including advertising, graphics, programming, writing, and translation. On any given day, the top-featured items might range from "I will record any Voice Over in a British accent" to "I will edit your cover letter" to the image of a shapely woman with a note that reads, "I will paint your logo or image on my back." The site has skyrocketed to become one of the 200 most popular websites in the world, and roughly 15 percent of Fiverr's sellers report the site as their main source of income. This rapid growth has inspired a group of venture capitalists to recently invest $15 million in the company.[2]

Kaufman believes you should fight a constant battle for simplicity. "We don't think simplicity is something you can do once." He explained to me, "As you introduce new features, you inherently make things more complex. So we are trying to add more features, but [we are] trying to make them available only to the advanced users."

THE POWER OF A NICHE

Fiverr itself also illustrates the ease with which you can develop new products and ideas. Trend Hunter terms this "instant entrepreneurship." It's never been easier to launch your business using

2   Alexa.com rank as of January 2013.

template website design, 3D printing to create prototypes, and the services offered by sites such as Fiverr. Today, a fourteen-year-old can craft a prototype, build a web presence, and start soliciting funds on Kickstarter long before the product is ready for sale. These simplified services all illustrate the potential of niche opportunities.

Niche ideas today have a far greater reach because the Internet helps you find similarly minded people. Launching a niche community can be done in the half hour it takes to start a Facebook fan page. Thousands of niche communities spring up on Facebook every day, many spiraling up in popularity and eventually becoming businesses in their own right.

My favorite online fan page is I F*cking Love Science, a shock-titled presentation that features weird animals, shocking facts, remixed Einstein pics, counterintuitive neuropsychology, and breakthrough science. In other words: fun science! It's a place where you might learn that "Scientists have found a way to implant false memories into mice." Or, you might explore the latest scientific breakthroughs, animal discoveries, and medical facts. Elise Andrew, a twenty-four-year-old Brit who studied biology in college, started the group in March 2012 to share science with her friends. Six months later, she'd earned a stunning 1 million fans and created a new mission: to showcase science in an "amusing and accessible way."[3]

A year later, Andrew's following surpassed 6 million fans, making I F*cking Love Science the world's most popular science fan group and launching Andrew into a related television project.

Fiverr and I F*cking Love Science teach us that in our new era of change and interconnectedness, you don't need to find a big idea; you can find a little idea that can be made big. Think of something

3   Elise Andrew, "I Fucking Love Science About Page," Facebook, retrieved August 7, 2013, https://www.facebook.com/IFeakingLoveScience/info.

fractional, smaller, simpler, or more focused—all with underlying growth potential.

But there are many forms of reduction, and sometimes this pattern is ideal for tackling a single, enormous business challenge.

FROM TAXIS TO TWEETS

Jack Dorsey was a shy little boy who loved trains, geography, computers, and listening to his police scanner. While the typical youth in his hometown of St. Louis may have decorated his walls with posters of action heroes and athletes, Dorsey plastered his room with maps. He dreamed of simplifying complex systems. In particular, he was fascinated by taxi dispatching, at the time a fractured process dominated by shortwave radio. Intrigued by the hive-like bursts of communication, he wondered if the antiquated process could be simplified.

Dorsey was only fourteen when he coded dispatching software for taxis, delivery fleets, and emergency vehicles. His software could plot dispatch vehicles onto maps, merging his two main interests: maps and taxi dispatch. And he was ready to put his genius to work. When you're fourteen and in search of an adult job, you need to take unconventional steps. So Dorsey hacked his way into the website of Dispatch Management Services Corp. Sneaking into the e-mail account of Greg Kidd, the company's founder, Dorsey wrote him an e-mail outlining how he could fix the operation's flaws. It was a risky move, but Dorsey was hired on the spot and went on to implement his dispatch software, which is still used by companies today.

Dorsey went on to code software in 2000 that would live-blog his location to friends. Unfortunately, his friends were not impressed (they couldn't imagine that Foursquare, the location-based website, would be a hit nine years in the future). The failure taught him something essential. To create a business based on simplicity, you need to solve a current problem.

Over the next few years, Dorsey appeared to drift. He worked as a nanny and as a masseuse and lived in the backyard shed of his former boss. But Dorsey was hunting. "Jack's top talent is not as a programmer. Yes, he can program and hack with the best of them," Kidd told the *Wall Street Journal*. "But his really startling quality is his social insights. He could study what Apple was hiring for in its job ads and predict what its next products and services would be with uncanny accuracy. He hacked an Internet browser so that you could see [what] people . . . had recently searched for."[4]

Dorsey was a pattern-seeker.

He started coding for Odeo, a podcasting start-up that was suddenly getting clobbered by competition from Apple. Feeling the pressure, Odeo's cofounder, Evan Williams, pushed the staff to brainstorm new product ideas. While sitting on a park bench, Dorsey was inspired by the idea of using text messaging to let people broadcast their messages. Williams loved the idea, and over the next few weeks, Dorsey and colleague Biz Stone coded the prototype. The team started using the software for internal communication and was convinced it had potential. In a day-long brainstorming session that included Dorsey, Williams, Stone, and a forth cofounder, Noah Glass, Twitter was born.

In October of 2006, the four approached investors with a plan to buy out the struggling Odeo and take their text messaging system to the next level. Twitter soon was attracting half a billion users based on a tremendously reductive approach to communication (not surprisingly, Dorsey's three guiding principles were simplicity,

---

4 Emily Maltby, "Punk Fan, Computer Hacker—Jack Dorsey's Early Years," *Wall Street Journal,* September 22, 2012, http://online.wsj.com/news/articles/SB10000872 396390444620104578008560821169192.

constraint, and craftsmanship). In just a few short years, Twitter went on to become a fundamental component of the technology ecosphere—a powerful new tool used by revolutionaries, marketers, Hollywood stars, presidents, and even the Pope. It's more than a novel way to connect people and ideas. Twitter has ushered in an iconic style of communication: short bursts riddled with acronyms and hashtags that never exceed the required limit of 140 characters.

But in 2008, Twitter unceremoniously booted Dorsey from his CEO position. His partners apparently felt that he was a better entrepreneur than a manager. Feeling not unlike Steve Jobs (also summarily ejected from a leadership role at an early age), Dorsey was crushed and had no idea what to do next.

FOURTH TIME'S A CHARM

As this book has repeatedly pointed out, failure can be a tremendous motivator, and it wasn't long before Dorsey seized on a new opportunity. One day, he was listening to his friend James McKelvey gripe. A recreational glass artist, McKelvey was frustrated because someone wanted to pay $2,000 for one of his pieces but McKelvey couldn't accept his credit card. Dorsey and McKelvey thought about how many other small vendors faced the same dilemma. This struck them as ironic, given the tremendous mobile computing power of iPhones.

That's all it took for Dorsey to prototype a product for yet another company. And not surprisingly, for this effort he once again utilized his favorite, proven opportunity pattern: simplify a terribly complicated system. In this case, he sought to simplify credit-card payments.

Thus, Square was born.

Dorsey and McKelvey realized that simplifying the acceptance of financial payments was a massive, international opportunity.

Setting up a merchant terminal is complicated and expensive, with some U.S. service contracts costing up to $10,000.[5] In contrast, Square would be remarkably simple. It wouldn't require installation or monthly fees. Just sign up online, and for no charge the company would send you a small square card reader that attaches to your iPhone. Download the free app, and you'd be ready to go.

Square makes it easy to take payments, whether you're a tradesperson, taxi driver, Craigslist seller, or Dorsey's mother (she was running a coffee shop). Interestingly, because he cared enough to think about his mom's modest needs, Dorsey added the analytics and reports missing in most traditional terminals. Most independent storekeepers and restaurants would be hard-pressed to tell you their day-end sales numbers. But Square provides full transparency in simple, easy-to-understand reports.

In 2013, after just three years in business, Square announced it was processing more than $15 billion in transactions on an annualized basis, making it one of the fastest-growing financial institutions in history.[6] The company quickly added a system to transform an iPad into a cash register, and it has announced plans for online payments.

In retrospect, Square is so simple and intuitive that you might have expected it to have been developed by a bank, credit card company, or online payment company. But suit-and-tie financial institutions are often bogged down by red tape, while the Jack Dorseys of the world train their sights on simplicity. Surf on over to the landing web pages of HSBC, Bank of America, or Wells Fargo,

---

5   Matt Warman, "Square Is the Shape of Things to Come, Says Twitter Founder Jack Dorsey," *Telegraph* (London), May 25, 2013, http://www.telegraph.co.uk/finance/ newsbysector/mediatechnologyandtelecoms/digital-media/10079532/Square-is-the -shape-of-things-to-come-says-Twitter-founder-Jack-Dorsey.html.

6   Om Malik, "With Square Stand, Jack Dorsey & Co. Reimagine the Cash Register," *Gigaom*, May 14, 2013.

and you'll find 818 words, 661 words, and 511 words, respectively.[7] By comparison, Square's landing page sports just sixty-nine words, including these: "Start accepting credit cards today. Sign up and we'll mail you a free Square Reader. 2.75% per swipe, no additional fees, and next day deposits."

Like Twitter, the Square website (and larger system) simplifies the complicated. In contrast, most financial institutions are preoccupied with offering customers a dizzying array of financial products.

Dorsey became a billionaire on paper in 2011, and the Twitter board wisely invited him back. He accepted the company's chairmanship, and the following year, the *Wall Street Journal* awarded him its "Innovator of the Year Award" for technology. Once again, Dorsey had created a useful solution by exploiting the same pattern: take complicated systems, boil them down to one key feature, and fashion a remarkably simple product.

Dorsey teaches us the importance of simplification, but he also shows us that a key step is starting with one thing you can do really well. For Square, that meant mobile payments. The caveat is that reduction can be a lot harder than it looks. "Making something simple is very difficult," Dorsey told *Vanity Fair* in a profile.[8] Today, Dorsey is known for routinely taking his teams on field trips to San Francisco's Lands End Park to marvel at the glorious Golden Gate Bridge. His purpose: to illuminate the bridge's awesome duality. Commuters depend on it every day, but when you look at it from afar, you're struck by its masterful design and elegance. Dorsey believes a good business should operate the same way, telling *SF Gate*, "When people come to Twitter and they want

---

7   Websites, retrieved August 11, 2013.

8   David Kirkpatrick, "Twitter Was Act One," *Vanity Fair,* April 2011, http://www .vanityfair.com/business/features/2011/04/jack-dorsey-201104.

to express something in the world, the technology fades away," he said. "It's them writing a simple message and them knowing that people will see it."[9]

SUB-PATTERNS OF REDUCTION

SIMPLIFICATION Our technological age has seen a general trend toward simplification. Websites have become more elegant and less cluttered, leading hardware firms are applauded for the features they leave out, and social media sites are increasingly minimalist. Even traditional product lines are benefiting from simplistic branding and design. In the beverage industry, for example, reality star Bethenny Frankel launched a line of simple martinis with fewer additives, carbs, and sugar. The drinks were specifically aimed at those on a diet who still want to party. Frankel sold her Skinnygirl Martinis brand for an estimated $64 million to Beam Global.

SPECIALIZATION Back in 2007, Trend Hunter started covering Europe's first "blow dry bars" for women who wanted their hair styled but not cut or colored. Later that year, the first North American blow dry bar, Blo, opened, quickly mushrooming to twenty-five locations. By 2012, competitor Drybar had also scaled up to twenty-five locations and captured $19 million in revenue, and the total for 2013 looks like it will be double.[10]

---

9   Alyson Shontell, "The Unusual Place Jack Dorsey Takes Employees to Motivate Them," *SF Gate*, March 18, 2013, Business Insider, http://www.sfgate.com/technology/businessinsider/article/The-Unusual-Place-Jack-Dorsey-Takes-Employees-To-4363340.php.

10 Kelsey Meany, "Blow Dry Bars Are a Thriving Industry Disrupting the Salon Business," *Daily Beast*, July 13, 2013, http://www.thedailybeast.com/articles/2013/07/13/blow-dry-bars-are-a-thriving-industry-disrupting-the-salon-business.html.

FEWER LAYERS AND STEPS Removing steps from a service has always been profitable, but it wasn't until the age of e-commerce and now social media that the tactic became so powerful. We've seen Zipcar, AutoShare, Car2Go, and others streamline rentals by making cars available by the hour, directly from lots. By forgoing rental car offices, these businesses did far more than reduce costs—they offered a more convenient customer experience.

FRACTIONAL From Airbnb, which allows homeowners to easily rent out their houses, to companies that allow customers to rent plants and art for their living space, fractional ownership is becoming an attractive way to sample luxury experiences. In California, Lyft raised more than $83 million in venture capital financing for an increasingly popular service that enables almost anyone to become a driver for hire. If you're already in a neighborhood where you see someone is looking for a ride, you can now rideshare in a more innovative way. To get better-than-taxi rates, passengers simply download an app and push a button that signals they want a rideshare. The result is an incredibly popular business model that is disrupting several traditional industries.

CROWDING Crowd-sourcing and crowd-funding have been pushing outside the boundaries of commerce, sometimes in startling ways. Kiva.org has raised billions by enabling people to fund individual farmers and basket-makers in developing countries. Indiegogo was used by Turkish youths to raise money for a full-page *New York Times* ad that brought attention to government oppression. And in Toronto, a crowd-funding campaign was used to purchase the infamous "crack video" that showed the city's mayor smoking crack. The video wasn't worth $200,000 to any *one* individual, but in a city of 6 million people, there were hundreds of thousands willing to pay a buck to see if the astonishing rumors were true. Unfortunately for Toronto, they were.

SUBSCRIPTION Business models that anticipate recurring sales, such as yearly subscriptions, are efficient for both company and customer, making them an excellent example of reduction. In 2012, Michael Dubin was peeved by the price of replacement razors and unconvinced that patented multi-blade technology was worth the premium. So he created a humorous video promoting his simple razor blades and offered a subscription service called Dollar Shave Club. (Much like with Fiverr, Dollar Shave's entry price of $1 a month is simply the starting point: The company also offers $6 and $9 monthly blade service.) Dubin's video, with its cheeky tagline "Our blades are f***king great" (something that would never fly with Gillette), attracted over ten million views, and by 2013, the club had 200,000 subscribers, generating an estimated $10 million in annual revenue.

MORE EFFICIENT Some of the biggest companies in finance and banking have earned their status through simplification, including ING Direct, eTrade, and Esurance. They all contradict the assumption that people need to visit physical branches to conduct business. By adopting an Internet-only approach, these companies were able to cut costs and grow into multibillion-dollar institutions.

SUMMARY: REDUCTION

This chapter has approached reductive opportunities from many different angles—from reality TV to the inspiration of personal failure to the potential for breakthrough technology innovations that border on genius. You've seen how key it is to feel pain and understand what lies behind it—to recognize and then skillfully remove the layers that can separate supply and demand. Reducing complexity, both in your product and your message, is essential to exploiting reductive patterns.

1. **Find a Little Idea** You don't need to find a big idea. You can also find a little idea that can be made big. That could mean something fractional, smaller, simpler, or more focused.

2. **Map Specific Pain Points** Most great ideas solve an existing problem. By thinking through the pains and problems of those in your niche, you can map out unique areas of opportunity.

3. **Remove the Layers That Separate Supply and Demand** The cost structure of a business is often bloated by markups charged by suppliers and middlemen. Identify the extra layers, and you can create value through simplification.

4. **Isolate Niche Pockets of People** It's become easier than ever to find niche pockets of similar-minded people. Josh Opperman, as we've seen, discovered a multimillion-dollar business in something as seemingly small as broken-hearted former fiancés.

5. **Be Number One (Even If It's in a Small Group or Category)** Being number one in a small market can lead to a deep connection with a homogeneous group of people who can become active ambassadors and open up a world of possibilities.

Chapter 10

ACCELERATION

ACCELERATION: Identifying a critical feature of a business or product and dramatically enhancing that element. Includes: perfection, aspirational positioning, exaggerated features, and reimagined solutions.

Acceleration is about taking an extreme position. It's about making an insightful observation about the marketplace and so boldly adapting your products in that direction that there's the risk of alienating some customers.

Often, the opportunity for acceleration stares at us for years but we don't dare push the limits far enough. In the auto world, for instance, hybrids have been with us since the 1997 launch of the Toyota Prius. By 2006, Americans were purchasing 200,000 hybrid vehicles a year.[1] While it was generally assumed that hybrid and electric cars would dominate in the near future, no modern major manufacturer had focused on building an all-electric car. Concerns about limited battery life and range kept automakers committed to the internal combustion engine. Defying the risks, Tesla took a bold gamble in 2008 and launched the Roadster, the first all-electric car. Five years later, it launched the Model S and won *Motor*

---

1   Bureau of Transportation Statistics, http://www.rita.dot.gov/bts/publications/pocket_guide_to_transportation/2013/environmental_sustainability/figure_05_04.

Trend's Car of the Year Award, which helped the company generate roughly $2 billion in annual revenue and pushed the company's stock to heady levels. Founder Elon Musk is now considered one of the world's greatest innovators.

The secret to acceleration is to recognize that the process may alienate a large proportion of consumers. For example, Panasonic realized in 1997 that broken laptops were causing corporations to lose hundreds of millions of dollars a year. The obvious solution was to make stronger laptops, but it became clear that durability would guarantee a certain amount of ugliness. What to do?

Like Dave Horvath of Uglydoll, the company decided to embrace ugly.

It launched rubber-coated, super-sized Panasonic Toughbooks. The devices lack aesthetic appeal, but not to the countless soldiers, field engineers, and oil rig workers who adore them. Mainstream consumers see them as clunkers, but Toughbooks trounce the competition when it comes to durability. Result? Panasonic has turned its rugged laptop product line into a billion-dollar annual business.

To profit from acceleration, you must be calculated and selective and take a distinct market position. Traditional companies often resign themselves to enhancing products along proven, past dimensions. If a company makes sexy dresses, it thinks only about how to make them sexier. This narrow path of optimization can ultimately lead to a company's undoing.

In this chapter, you'll learn how to create far more intense, superior versions of existing products. We'll also explore methods for developing unique ideas that can be expanded into new markets.

TURNING MUD PUDDLES INTO OPPORTUNITIES

Picture this: You're dripping sweat, covered in mud, and surrounded by a screaming, grimacing mob of men and women who, like you, are wading through bogs, leaping into ice-filled Dumpsters, dart-ing through walls of fire, and racing through a maze of live electric wires. It may seem as if you've wandered into a war zone, but people really do *pay* to endure this torture. Welcome to Will Dean's Tough Mudder, a torturous adventure course that demonstrates the accel-eration pattern.

Before Tough Mudder, Dean spent several years in Britain's For-eign and Commonwealth Office working in the office of counter-terrorism. By 2007, he was feeling entrepreneurial and departed for America to earn an MBA at Harvard while independently studying the business of adventure.

Endurance racing has thrived for over a quarter-century, dating back to the first 1978 Iron Man, an annual 140-mile triathlon held in Hawaii. But Dean couldn't help noticing that for most runners triathlons, ultramarathons, and road races weren't about the activity per se: "The thing I really disliked about triathlons and marathons," he explained to the *New York Times*, "was that the only real arbiter of how well you did was your time."[2] The emphasis on time created an imbalance that implied one winner, thousands of losers, and, generally, a big gap between your performance and the handful of elite contestants.

Dean wanted to create a race that accelerated the feeling of accomplishment, so he banished the time clock. He noticed that adrenaline-fueled sports had become increasingly intertwined with pop culture. The X Games was an early pioneer, and *The Amazing Race, Survivor,* and *Wipeout* were successful reality TV programs. Even the organizers of the Winter Olympics had introduced riskier sports such as ski cross, half-pipe, and short-track speed skating. Teen beverage advertising had dramatically shifted from Coca-Cola Classic to adrenaline brands such as 5-hour ENERGY, Red

---

2   John Branch, "Playing with Fire, Barbed Wire and Beer," *New York Times*, April 28, 2010, http://www.nytimes.com/2010/04/29/sports/29mudder.html?page wanted=all&_r=0.

Bull, Monster Energy, and Rockstar. Red Bull's wacky Flugtag ("flight day") promotion demonstrated the humorous side of this devil-may-care trend. Contestants built themed "flying machines" and then flew (or, more accurately, plummeted) off a raised platform into water.

Against this shifting backdrop, Dean spotted an opportunity. He set out to accelerate obstacle racing, a sport already gaining traction in Europe with Britain's The Grim Challenge and Germany's Strongman Run. What's interesting is that Dean was late to the party. Tough Guy, an event that prides itself on the likelihood of racers getting "cuts, scrapes, burns, dehydration, hypothermia, acrophobia, claustrophobia, electric shocks, sprains, twists, joint dislocation and broken bones," was already in its twenty-seventh year.[3] Dean saw this landscape and set out to design an even more intense adventure experience in which people were less likely to compare their times and more likely to say, "Wasn't the electrocution pit awesome?!"

He envisioned a ten- to twelve-mile military-style adventure, designed by British Special Forces for added bragging rights. Mud-splattered contestants would slog and dash and slide their way through challenges that would include barbed wire, rope climbs, and, yes, even possible electrocution. He planned to ditch event clocks and prizes. Finishers would be greeted by a cold beer and an epic bash. Participants wouldn't compare their completion times. Simply participating and surviving was the goal.

Dean proposed his plan at the 2009 Harvard Business School Case Competition. Though he was a finalist, his idea failed to win the top award of the judges, who warned that he wouldn't find 500 people in America willing to sign up for such self-torture.

Undaunted, Dean teamed up with Guy Livingston, a longtime

---

3   "Tough Guy January 26th 2014 Promotion Material," Tough Guy Website, retrieved May 11, 2013, https://eventdesq.imgstg.com/index.cfm?fuseaction =main&EventDesqID=1702&OrgID=2107.

friend also seeking an entrepreneurial adventure. With just a six-person team, a modest $8,000 marketing budget, and an aggressive Facebook campaign, they scheduled their first event at the Bear Creek Ski Resort in 2010. The response was phenomenal. More than 4,500 participants signed up, each paying over $100 to join the torture.

Bales of burning straw, ice water, and grueling muddy bogs challenged the competitors. Finishers were greeted with beer, convivial celebration, and the ubiquity of the Tough Mudder label. Tattoo artists were on hand to tattoo the Tough Mudder brand onto competitors' bodies, and barbers waited at the finish line, ready to give free mohawks or mullets.

The rough-and-tumble bonding experience was shared widely and rapidly, and it quickly accelerated. By the end of the first year, two more events (Bear Valley, California, and Englishtown, Pennsylvania) attracted 4,000 and then 9,300 participants. Tough Mudder expanded to fifteen events in 2011, and thirty-five in 2012. Within two years, Tough Mudder grew into a $70 million company.[4]

Since then, more than a million Tough Mudder participants have signed up for the torture. During a recent keynote, I mentioned Tough Mudder, and an attendee limped up afterward with a big smile and said, "Check this out. Do you see my space boot? I've been in it for five weeks since snapping my Achilles tendon at a Tough Mudder." I didn't know whether I should console him or congratulate him, until he exclaimed, "Wanna know the best part? I'm signed up to do another in September!"

A critic might argue that Dean didn't invent adventure races. But his creation has been the most successful of all the new adventure races because of how smartly he exploited several *acceleration* opportunities.

---

4   Tim Donelly, "Zooming from Zero to $70 million in 2 Years," *Inc.*, March 29, 2012.

Dean not only intensified the human challenge and fed people's fascination with the extreme, he built a tribe out of it. Instead of continuing on the dull and diminishing path of ever-longer running races, his event celebrated spectacular and unique challenges involving ice baths and fire.

Dean also smartly focused on making his adventure practical and rewarding. Most extreme sports require too much aerobic training or focus too much on competition itself. Tough Mudder has no time clock. It's more about *completing* rather than measuring your performance. Participants are encouraged to tackle a Tough Mudder in a spirit of camaraderie, helping their fellow participants throughout the course.

Finally, Dean capitalized on the desire to share using social media. He ensured that Tough Mudder's military-style obstacles were professionally photographed, giving competitors plenty of ammunition for their Facebook pages and blogs. The event is *designed* to "go viral." Tough Mudders become authentic advocates of the brand.

So far, three adventure race start-ups have taken off—Warrior Dash, a shorter event that brings in $50 million in annual revenue; Spartan Series, which generates $30 million; and, of course, Tough Mudder.[5] As you might expect, the entrepreneurs behind these businesses are fierce competitors. Lawsuits, countersuits, and allegations of stolen ideas, copyright infringement, and defamation of character have piled up.

Exploiting these opportunities is not for the fainthearted. Entrepreneurs planning to accelerate need to be prepared for rough-and-tumble competition. But beyond the scrapes and bruises, the potential rewards are high. The astonishing success of Tough Mudder and two other obstacle course start-ups is proof that acceleration—both literal and figurative—can be very profitable.

---

5   Scott Keneally, "Playing Dirty," *Outside,* October 22, 2012, http://www.out sideonline.com/outdoor-adventure/multisport/Playing-Dirty-November-2012.html? page=1.

TOUGH GIRLS WEAR SKIRTS

Nicole DeBoom, a professional triathlete, was running through her town one dreary cold December day when she spied her reflection in a store window. Her heart sank when she realized that her traditional running gear made her resemble a boy. It was a shock. She hadn't realized until then how running shorts can make women look and feel masculine.

Suddenly, she knew what she had to do: "If I could be in touch with my 'pretty' image," she told me, "I could be more motivated to run."

DeBoom dashed home and quickly scribbled down the word "pretty" and then "women's clothing that makes you look and feel good." Brainstorming led to the concept of a running skirt, a potent new symbol of femininity—and one that was ahead of its time.

Just like that, DeBoom threw herself into designing and prototyping running skirts. Nine months later, in September of 2004, DeBoom stood on top of the Ironman Wisconsin awards podium, having captured the $5,000 prize while racing in a skirt. She poured her winnings into her entrepreneurial efforts, and the following year, she brought her first stockpile of running skirts to the Austin Marathon. They quickly sold out. *Runner's World* featured her design in an article titled "Tough Girls Wear Skirts." DeBoom's company, Skirt Sports, was off and running, and she quickly sold 2,500 skirts in a few months.

But running skirts were also polarizing. "I had love notes and hate mail," DeBoom told me. "Some women felt it was a shame that we should care what we look like. Others would say that they wished [the skirt] came out ten years ago." DeBoom thought all the noise was a sign that she was onto something big. "We created something controversial, and that could only help us."

Why was her idea so hot? DeBoom successfully identified an

aspect of competitive running ripe for acceleration—women's desire to not have their femininity obscured by their running clothing. By creating a product that tapped into the desire for athletic women to still want to flaunt a feminine appearance, she launched a provocative new category of sporting apparel.

In a bid to further accelerate her business, in 2007 DeBoom launched a 5k race called Convert to Skirt. Competitors later dubbed it the "Skirt Chaser 5k," and the name stuck. The "Skirts" (women) get a head start, and three minutes later, the men give chase. There's a big party after the race, with music, drinks, and mingling (singles are asked to wear a sticker, which helps turn the event into a giant mixer). The race was a hit—and sparked instant controversy. College newspapers, DeBoom recalled, "started blasting [Skirt Sports] as a sexist company and calling the Skirt Chaser 'one step back' for the women's rights movement." Feminist groups attacked DeBoom, calling the word "chase" predatory.

DeBoom told me that in subsequent Skirt Chasers, she subtly shifted her messaging to emphasize love and relationships. Also, she redesigned her logo, making it "stronger rather than sexier," and adjusted her marketing to point out that the women are in charge: "Women start first and 'invite the men to join us.'"[6] Thankfully, the ultracompetitive DeBoom hasn't taken her foot off the accelerator. Today, the Skirt Chaser 5k is a six-city phenomenon with races in the United States and Canada. And the company's website continues to take risks, featuring a silhouette of a woman posing provocatively in a running skirt with the tease "Your Pace or Mine?"

At Trend Hunter, we've noticed that niche clothing is a growing wave, and we see much more opportunity in this vein. Other examples that we've spotted include gloves made of conductive materials for easy smartphone use, high heels with collapsible heels for

---

6   Mario Schulzke, "Nicole DeBoom—Owner of Skirt Sports," *Idea Mensch*, October 9, 2012, http://ideamensch.com/nicole-deboom.

driving, solar-powered handbags for phone charging, snowboard helmets with built-in headphones, and wellness watches to track athletic activity. Each of these products has succeeded by specifically focusing on a narrow purpose—then fast-tracking it.

RACE AGAINST THE MACHINE

Picture this scenario involving a woman I'll call Julie. She's a young single mother, playing with her toddler Alexis at a sunny suburban park in Dallas. Out of the blue, she gets a text from a familiar number. "It's hard to believe that Alexis is already two! Do you want to know when and how to start saving for school?"

Julie texts back "yes," and she quickly receives a phone call.

The familiar voice offers some helpful information and advice: "By the time Alexis is nineteen, with inflation in education, her post-secondary education could cost $300,000, assuming she stays in Texas. Do you want to know how to save for that?" Julie says yes, and she is told, "If your account earns 5 percent, you'll need to save $215 a week, which you have the budget for, based on your salary, expenses, and inflation." Just then, Julie sees that her mom is phoning. She drops the call with the bank and forgets about it.

Later that weekend, she logs into her bank account. A chat window pops up, continuing the earlier conversation: "Did you want me to set up an account and start withdrawing $215?" With the click of a button, Julie agrees.

What's surprising—or maybe *not* so surprising—about this scenario is that the intelligence behind the texts and voice is not Julie's trusted financial advisor. The "voice" on the other side of the text isn't even human. In this scenario, Julie is texting and chatting with Watson, the IBM supercomputer famous for challenging *Jeopardy!* champions Brad Rutter and Ken Jennings in February of 2010. That battle of machine against man was a milestone in computer engineering, and it foreshadowed how Watson would be adapted for far greater purposes, such as saving lives in hospitals and planning financial futures.

Watson's backstory is a decade-long adventure in experimenting and tapping into the power of acceleration. I had a rare chance to meet with Watson's creators when I spoke at IBM's Smarter Commerce Conference, where Watson was first unveiled. Stephen Gold, a dark-haired, excitable vice president responsible for commercializing the project, let me in on the intriguing backstory.

ACCELERATION ROUND 1: TURNING A GAME INTO A SPECTACLE

During the Cold War, the Soviets and Americans turned chess into a battleground for proving intellectual superiority. The Soviets funded and trained legions of players, creating a veritable "chess machine," and the Americans used prize money and publicity to compete.

Given that dramatic context, when IBM wanted to prove the power of its technology, it chose chess as the playing field. The company knew that computers were increasingly capable of amazing things, but it needed to accelerate that point—it needed to do something bold and newsworthy that would convince skeptics.

The company hired a team of brilliant scientists who would spend eight years on a single-minded mission: to engineer the ultimate chess-playing robot. When the machine, named "Deep Blue," was finally ready for battle, IBM offered Soviet Garry Kasparov—the man many consider to be the best player ever—a huge sum to face off against it.

Kasparov, sixteen-time world champion, confidently accepted the challenge. With the world watching, Deep Blue won the first game, but it went on to lose the match. Man beat machine, but by the following year, IBM had readied a new model for a rematch, aptly named Deeper Blue. In the second match, the computer made a simple mistake, but Kasparov overthought his opponent, attributing the mistake to supreme intelligence, and Deeper Blue narrowly beat Kasparov.

Kasparov demanded another shot, delivering a public challenge in *Time* magazine: "I think IBM owes me, and all mankind, a rematch."[7] The company refused, and Deeper Blue was dismantled. IBM later claimed the event—religiously covered by network news and top newspapers—was worth hundreds of millions in publicity.

Deeper Blue taught IBM that accelerating a specific challenge can deliver a phenomenal result. IBM accomplished many technological feats in that same decade, but it was Deeper Blue that symbolized the company's brand, created a sense of purpose for employees, and provided a dynamic, highly public framework for the ongoing battle between man and machine.

The thinking behind the development of Deep Blue relates directly to the subject of this book. Just as the computer was able to beat the world's most brilliant human chess master by understanding patterns, you can study patterns to make sense of the chaos around you and spot the opportunities others can't see.

ACCELERATION ROUND 2: BUILDING CURIOSITY WITH AN EPIC CHALLENGE

Seven years after the creation of Deeper Blue, IBM's research manager, Charles Lickel, was dining with some coworkers when the clamor of the noisy restaurant suddenly ebbed. Everyone stared at the TVs placed throughout the restaurant to see if *Jeopardy!* champion Ken Jennings would win another game. Jennings was in the middle of a seventy-four-game winning streak that was bringing

---

7   Garry Kasparov, "IBM Owes Mankind a Rematch," *Time,* May 26, 1997.

the game show back to the forefront of pop culture. Lickel was reminded of the aura that surrounded the chess matches. What if IBM could take Deeper Blue to the next level and defeat Ken Jennings at *Jeopardy!*?

To win a game show, the new computer needed to think broadly about patterns and learn like a human. It would have to understand complicated language, innuendo, and subtleties of language that no computer had yet been able to master. The team couldn't use traditional programming, where one might code a million different rules and decision trees for the computer to follow. That volume of coding would be impossible. Instead, the team members would expose the machine to every piece of available information. Incredibly, they'd teach it to learn on its own by looking for patterns.

When I spoke with Gold, he explained the nature of the challenge by comparing this new machine, Watson, to Google: "The problem with search, and we've all done this, is that with search, you get four million hits, you look at the top two or three and then you put new keywords in." Google is essentially farming an answer. In contrast, Watson must hunt.

If you ask, "What is two plus two?" almost anyone will tell you "four," including Google. Watson, however, needs to answer, "It depends. To an automotive engineer, two plus two could be a car configuration: two front seats, two back seats. To a family psychologist, two plus two could be a family unit: two parents, two children. To a gambler, two plus two is a poker strategy."

After several years of intensive work, the pattern-based approach to learning resulted in Watson being able to play *Jeopardy!*—at least well enough to defeat internal IBM staffers. The machine soon knew every past *Jeopardy!* question, the entire text of Wikipedia, an entire dictionary, volumes of pop culture information, scientific texts, and even the complete Urban Dictionary. But understanding slang could be tricky. In a humorous encounter, when IBM first showcased Watson, the machine rang the buzzer and blurted out,

"F*ck you." For the team, that public insult hurt because it was a glaring example of just how wrong Watson could be.

Like many innovators struggling with a tough problem, the team kept falling into the traps of the farmer, seeking to repeat what had worked well in the past: "Every time we hit a roadblock or obstacle, we almost went back to the core of what we knew from the programmatic days," he explained to me. "We'd say, 'Oh, we'll just build a rule for that.'" The whole team could see that progress was being made, but team members were often tempted to take short-cuts by fashioning new rules. Yet, as Gold says, that was a trap they had to avoid: "Unless prescriptively a situation comes up exactly as you conceive it, rules aren't going to work well."

The team "had to completely evolve out of the notion of using old rules." As he explained this to me, I realized they were putting into practice something very similar to one of my favorite mantras: break rules! There's nothing that prevents companies from success-fully innovating more than the very rules they put in place to pro-tect the status quo.

After seven more years of absorbing knowledge and learning patterns, Watson was ready for prime time. In a televised match, the machine appeared on *Jeopardy!* to challenge former champions Brad Rutter and Ken Jennings, who had his seventy-four-game winning streak to protect.[8] Watson's near-instant access to 200 mil-lion pages of content made the machine a very speedy know-it-all. Jennings won $24,000 and Rutter $21,600, but the computer dom-inated the human contenders with $77,147 in earnings. A humble Jennings noted in his Final Jeopardy! response, "I, for one, welcome our new computer overlords."

Like the Deeper Blue conquest, the feat triggered global public-ity and a resurgence of client interest in IBM. But what could the

---

8   "Jeopardy! and IBM Announce Charities to Benefit from Watson Competi-tion," IBM Website, January 13, 2011, http://www-03.ibm.com/press/us/en/pressre lease/33373.wss.

company do outside of beating chess masters and *Jeopardy!* champions?

ACCELERATION ROUND 3: THE CHESS GAME OF CHANGING THE WORLD

What do you do with a machine that can win *Jeopardy!*? Gold recalled to me, "We didn't know until we actually got to *Jeopardy!* what the actual commercial opportunities might be." Hundreds of potential paths beckoned, but each was a bit of a stretch. The team narrowed in on Watson's strengths: processing high volumes of information, understanding language, and learning. This led IBM to health care. Perhaps Watson could help diagnose illness or assist in the search for medical cures. The catch was that health care is even more complicated than *Jeopardy!* Gold explained, "It's like saying, 'I just got my driver's license—I think I will race in Formula One next year.' It's a great thing to try to do . . . but it's really hard."

However, when the team learned that one in five medical diagnoses is wrong or incomplete, they were motivated. Instead of filling up Watson's memory with innumerable trivia questions and world facts, they poured in medical studies, facts, and patient records. Imagine having a doctor with a brain packed with the near sum total of knowledge about medicine—every combination of symptoms matched to every combination of family history, risk factor, and potential diagnosis.

Today, Watson is being deployed in certain hospitals—not as a doctor yet, but as a diagnostic machine. IBM reports that at New York City's Memorial Sloan Kettering Cancer Center, 90 percent of the center's nurses follow Watson's guidance, combining their human judgment with the precision and efficiency of a machine.[9]

---

9   Bruce Upbin, "IBM's Watson Gets Its First Piece of Business in Healthcare," *Forbes*, February 8, 2013, http://www.forbes.com/sites/bruceupbin/2013/02/08/ibms-watson-gets-its-first-piece-of-business-in-healthcare.

Earlier, I gave an example of one of the ways that Watson is making its presence felt in finance—by helping mothers and fathers open education savings accounts for their children. Remember Julie? That scenario and technology are real, and today, IBM is partnering with several banks, including RBC Financial, to help prove the business value of computer-assisted financial planning.

Watson is proving the power of patterns. IBM originally expected that each Watson implementation would need to be a special case. But Gold explains that the company is learning that pattern opportunity is much broader: "What we've uncovered is that the types of interactions that organizations and individuals have are not that different. If you look at a lawyer relative to a doctor, someone might say that those are different patterns. But what does a lawyer do? He evaluates case law. He researches precedents, and examines the facts of the case and the stories of witnesses. That sounds a lot like what doctors do. . . . The psychology is different, but the pattern is the same."

Based on Gold's words, we can see that Watson's ethos is this book's ethos. From fashion to tech to finance, patterns have the potential to shortcut an individual's way to success.

SUB-PATTERNS OF ACCELERATION

PERFECTION Creating a perfect product is more complicated and expensive than creating one that is simply great. Companies typically respond by striking a balance between quality and price. However, there are some instances in which perfection can pay off. For example, over the past few decades, there have been modest enhancements to competitive swimsuits, but leading up to the 2008 Olympic Games, Speedo decided on a radically accelerated strategy. The company teamed with NASA to create the ultimate swimsuit. The fruit of that extraordinary collaboration was the LZR, an ultrasonically welded, full-body, lightweight swimsuit fashioned from a futuristic fabric. The swimsuit was so over-engineered that athletes wearing it set thirteen world records within a month of its release. During the 2008 Olympics, 98 percent of medal winners wore the suit, and of the twenty-five Olympic swimming records set, twenty-three were achieved by swimmers wearing the LZR. The super swimsuit was subsequently banned from future Olympics, but its otherworldly success created a halo around the Speedo brand.[10]

ASPIRATIONAL ICON Many companies strive to create a high-performance version of a product to draw consumers over time toward that more expensive alternative. In the auto industry, for example, the highest-performing model often achieves iconic status. Though many customers initially buy an entry-level model, a large percentage often trade up to the higher-margin product. This "lure them in" strategy has been highly successful in many industries— for example, in the computer chip business with Intel. In the 1990s, consumers clearly wanted more speed, so Intel invested heavily to make sure it always had the fastest chips, and it then heavily advertised that it had achieved "state of the art." This caused consumers to crave machines branded with the "Intel Inside" logo, and the preference allowed Intel to charge a massive price premium over chips from rival AMD. Result? Intel remained the market leader even though at any given time most consumers weren't buying the fastest Intel chips.

EXAGGERATED FEATURE Pick a feature or an attribute that will allow your company, product, or brand to be the best. Then draw attention

---

10 Record Breaking Benefit, NASA, http://www.nasa.gov/offices/oct/home/tech_record_breaking.html#.UquJLeIg_70.

to that feature. For example, Blendtec has a powerful blender. To rise above the competition, the company created a YouTube series titled "Will It Blend." Each week, the company takes something people are talking about, such as the latest iPhone or consumer product, and tosses it into their near-industrial-strength kitchen blender. Yes, it's dramatic storytelling—the machine grinding is visual proof that the Blendtec is an awe-inspiring blender. In the first year of the channel, Blendtec's sales grew sixfold, and by the end of 2013, the channel had garnered over 230 million views.

REIMAGINED SOLUTION Innovators can ignite passion and excitement in an otherwise dull industry through a reimagined solution. For example, household vacuuming was considered dull until James Dyson rethought how vacuums work. Frustrated by the clogging vacuum bag in his own home, Dyson worked to create a new solution. Recalling a trip to a windmill, he remembered seeing the stirring wind create mini cyclones that stirred wood chips on the floor into a neat little pile in the middle of the room. He wondered if that same cyclone-like movement could be applied to home vacuum cleaners. So he set about refining an idea, creating 5,127 vacuum cleaner prototypes before arriving at one that would perfectly produce a similar effect. In 1991, he launched an accelerated version of the Dyson vacuum that would win the International Design Fair and eventually become the world's standard for powerful, high-end, well-designed vacuum cleaners.

SUMMARY: ACCELERATION

Acceleration is both easy and difficult. Certainly, we're used to competing by making something bigger, faster, or better, but it's critical to choose the right feature to accelerate.

TAKEAWAYS

1. **Pinpoint Why Something Is Great** To accelerate an idea, pinpoint the feature people enjoy the most, and then set out to improve that feature. As we've seen, in creating Tough Mudder, Will Dean amplified the sense of accomplishment one feels after surviving a torturous endurance event.

2. **Create Distance from the Competition** To create something remarkable, it's critical to be perceived as significantly different. For Will Dean, that meant accelerating the idea of accomplishment by constructing a race that was crammed full of extreme threats—from fire to electrocution.

3. **You Can Accelerate Something Small** You don't need to build something as massive as a Tough Mudder. Simply find an idea or your inspiration and take it to the next level with a product or service that fully engages a consumer need.

4. **Take an Emotion or Idea and Emphasize It** Running made Nicole DeBoom feel feminine and pretty, but her attire didn't. So she zeroed in on that aspect and designed a running skirt that would help her feel dramatically more feminine.

5. **Create Epic Challenges** Challenges can inspire great things. With Deep Blue and Deeper Blue, IBM challenged itself to develop a machine that could win at the highest levels of chess. Then, with Watson, the task was to produce a machine capable of "out-

thinking" humans and winning *Jeopardy!* That technology now promises to kick off a new artificial-intelligence-accelerated era in medicine, business, and science. As for the company itself, today it boasts over one billion dollars in annual revenue.

SUMMARY OF THE PATTERNS OF OPPORTUNITY

Through remarkable examples of success, you've learned how nerds, ex-cons, fashionistas, and entrepreneurs-at-heart have leveraged the six patterns of opportunity to create breakthrough products and services. In the next section, we'll dive deeper into how you can actually apply the patterns and make them work for your industry.

The Six Patterns

1. Convergence—combining previously unrelated products and services.

2. Divergence—diverging from the mainstream (to achieve status or to customize).

3. Cyclicality—following cycles that are predictable among generations or that recur in history, fashion, or economics.

4. Redirection—shifting, repurposing, or repositioning a concept.

5. Reduction—the simplification, specialization, or micro-targeting of an idea.

6. Acceleration—identifying a critical feature and dramatically enhancing it.

Part III

Capture

Chapter 11

THE HUNTING GROUND

rmed with a knowledge of the patterns of opportunity and having awakened your inner hunter, you're now better prepared to
spot and hit those opportunities to find better ideas, faster.

First, you need to narrow your focus. Develop this skill and
you'll be able to zero in on the opportunities that are just big
enough to be profitable, but not so large and obvious that your
competitors can already spot them. It starts with learning how to
intelligently narrow the range of what you're looking at. Here's a
framework for how:

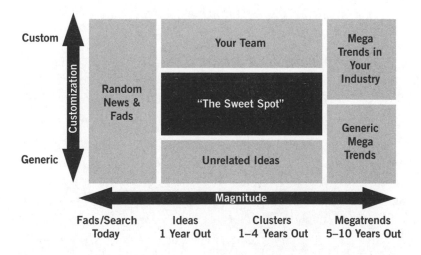

NARROWING YOUR FOCUS

1. **Not Too Big** Most people have already been buried by media coverage of such megatrends as eco, social media, and the rise of China. To spot something profitable, you need to dig deeper into smaller, less-obvious opportunities that match your advantages and talents.

2. **Not Too Small** The word *trend* often gets misused to define what is surging on Twitter or Google. These little fads can be fascinating, but their time in the spotlight is fleeting. They aren't significant enough to generate a long-lasting competitive advantage.

3. **Not What You Know** When you hunt, you need to avoid spending too much time on the trends and ideas you've already spotted. These trends will seem to pop out at you because of your brain's innate tendency to farm the same ground.

THE POWER OF A CLUSTER

The key to digging up great business ideas is to find a cluster of opportunity. A cluster is a group of products, services, or concepts that follows a similar idea. Clusters are important because they signify consumer interest in something far broader than a single product. Find a great cluster, and you'll then be tapping into a deep consumer need or opportunity that can be satisfied with multiple products.

For example, if you look at the beverage market over the last couple decades, it's easy to see in retrospect how dramatically the landscape has changed. Red Bull, as we've discussed, was the divergent innovator, creating a tremendous lifestyle brand that was powered by extreme adventure. The company took caffeine, the core drug in coffee seeds, and masterfully transformed it into an experience. Red Bull took something old and made it new. A full fifteen years after Red Bull's launch, Monster Energy Drink jumped into the business, and since then, it has emerged as a close second in revenue and reputation. Rockstar Energy, which launched in 2002, is the other player to gain significant market share (about 10 percent in the United States).

Amazingly, the major soda conglomerates were late to the energy drink game. These dominant companies focused only on uncaffeinated beverages in the 1990s and early years of this century, missing the next big caffeine pattern. Yes, there were ample opportunities for specialty coffee, but the bigger new territory—and cluster—was taking coffee places it hadn't gone before. The Indiana company Living Essentials saw the pattern. Its 5-hour ENERGY shots essentially shrank the already diminutive Red Bull can into a single two-ounce gulp. It accelerated Red Bull, as expressed in the tagline "Drink it in seconds, feel it in minutes." Similarly, Gu Energy Labs of Berkeley, California, was one of several companies that created a way to quickly ingest caffeine with carbs and sugar—in this case, via tiny gel packs. Today, there are countless candy-like morsels—from capsules to potato chips—that are essentially caffeine-delivery systems. Together, these products signify a cluster of opportunity, which at Trend Hunter we call "caffeine ubiquity."

In 2011, a group of longtime coworkers and friends from the consumer packaged goods business spotted this same opportunity and decided to pursue it in a start-up, which they called Awake. Building off the caffeine ubiquity cluster, they focused on charging up chocolate bars with caffeine. In less than two years, they developed a few different caffeinated chocolate treats and quickly gained media attention. "We could see from these multiple examples that people wanted something caffeinated that was not coffee, and we realized many of those people were teenagers," co-founder Matt Schnarr told me. By 2014, Awake had developed a broad range of products, from chocolate bars to caramel chocolates to single-serving squares, which it was pushing out to 20,000 convenience stores and 1,300 campus stores. "When you find an insight, and not just a single little idea, it gives you something bigger that you can build off of."

The Awake team didn't try to market yet another energy drink. They'd been watching the tsunami of non-coffee caffeinated products grow and jumped in with a novel concept that rode the momentum of a very hot cluster.

As you'll see later in this chapter, this kind of opportunity is available in all sorts of industries.

LET'S CREATE A BUSINESS

Imagine that you've come up with a promising new entrepreneurial idea that you want to give wings to. Maybe it's a service or product that you're developing yourself, or maybe you're taking it to a major company. You'd like to launch it in a retail store, but your budget is limited. Then imagine that your business partner suggests a pop-up shop. Since you can't possibly afford a full store, it seems like a brilliant idea. But when you get around to actually designing and building a pop-up, you're confused.

There are so many possibilities that it's easy to get off track.

Before reading the next section, take a few minutes to think about and visualize your pop-up. Where would it be located? What would you sell? What would the limited space look and feel like?

The reason I've asked you to go through this exercise is that it demonstrates our natural limitations. When we try to innovate on the fly, our first ideas will almost always be rooted in gut instinct and offhand perceptions of pop-up shops. These early ideas will often be too grand or too generic to be useful. This pop-up shop exercise will help you see how trend-spotting and clustering can help refine your idea into something more exciting and focused.

Here's how it works. Whether I'm helping Cadbury to develop a new type of chocolate or Microsoft to rethink its future, my trend-spotting workshops tend to follow seven battle-tested steps:

STEP 1: AWAKEN YOUR HUNTER. Think about all I've told you regarding the hunter versus the farmer and the importance of breaking free from your gut instinct. To find a remarkable *new* idea, you need a fresh way of thinking. For many innovators, this can be accomplished by looking outside their industry for inspiration. A good example was on display in my surprising interview with Marco Morosini, one of Ferrari's top designers. I expected him to tell me that he scouted for new ideas by frequenting all the auto shows, studying every type of motorsport, and paying close attention to how street racers modify their cars. Instead, he told me that he spent half his work hours designing women's fashions. Even though Ferrari is one of the world's most macho carmakers, Morosini believes that the only way he can stay fresh and inspired is to explore many different realms. He told me, "You need to be more open to the complete possibility of what could be."

STEP 2: ESTABLISH A HUNTING GROUND. As a starting point, you'll want to actively hunt all of the similar ideas in your market. Being aware of innovations in your market will inspire an idea based on the best of everything that has happened before. You might find these ideas by searching online, traveling, interviewing people, or reading books, magazines, and trade publications in your category. And of course, TrendHunter.com was intentionally structured to be a wellspring of inspiration, so you're welcome to search our free database of 250,000 ideas, which, as you'll see, will open your mind to a range of possibilities.

Note that each of these trend-based examples is real, so if you'd like to dive deeper and explore each example, visit BetterandFaster.com/popups.

FIRST ROUND OF IDEAS: POP-UP SHOPS

Pop-Up Party Buses

Square Enix brought the "Final Fantasy" video game to life with school buses turned into arcades.

Fold-Away Fashion Stores

The 24 Issey Miyake store could easily be "stored" away, making it usable anywhere.

Virtual Subway Supermarkets

Homeplus created billboards featuring pictures of food you could order from your phone.

Indoor Garden Exhibits

The Openhouse Gallery was a pop-up art exhibit staged in a city park.

Art Gallery Fashion Pop-Up

The Lightbox Shop for Schwarzkopf was a Karl Lagerfeld–designed art and fashion gallery.

Billboard Libraries

The Billboard Library enabled you to loan out new books by simply scanning their QR Code on a billboard.

Coffee Shop Pop-Up Banks

ING created an express mobile coffee bar that also offered banking.

Pop-Up Roller Rinks

UNIQLO sparked attention with a pop-up roller rink.

Pop-Up Dinner Parties

One thousand people gathered wearing white for "Dîner en Blanc" in New York City.

Pedal-Powered Portable Movie Theaters

Cycle-In Cinema is an impromptu outdoor movie theater that requires people power.

Temporary Monumental Pop-Ups

The Cube pop-up from Electrolux looked like a giant French castle.

Shipping Container Sports Stores

Puma's pop-up shop allowed the brand to quickly expand on time for the World Cup.

STEP 3: SEARCH THE PERIMETER FOR SLIGHTLY RELATED IDEAS. Expand your viewpoint to include concepts that aren't iterations of what you intend but are related enough to be inspiring. Instead of just looking at existing stores, you could track in-store retail innovations, the art of window displays, and unique new vending machines. These clever approaches are obviously not pop-up shops, but they share a similar goal of trying to capture the retail shopper's attention, often through some technique that can perhaps make its way into your business. By examining what's adjacent to your business challenge, you'll find yourself leaping mentally to new possibilities. Take, for example, the following:

SLIGHTLY RELATED IDEAS: IN-STORE INNOVATION, UNIQUE STOREFRONTS, VENDING MACHINES

Sci-Fi Retail Centers

The L'atoll Angers shopping mall is inspired by the future.

Optical Illusion Openings

For its flagship store in Chicago, Burberry created an illusion of infinity.

Motion-Activated Ads

Perception interactive billboards respond to observer interactions.

Facial ID Vending

The Sanden vending machine customizes offerings based on your face.

Movie Theater Couture Shops

The Louis Vuitton "Roma Etoile" boutique has its own movie theater.

Furniture Store Slumber Parties

IKEA's sleepover went viral with unexpected fun and pampering.

Scannable Product Deliveries

Walmart and P&G's PGMobile trucks offer convenience and accessibility.

3D Retail Shopping Walls

The adiVerse virtual footwear wall offers shoppers the ultimate retail therapy.

Bartering Vending Machines

The Swap-O-Matic allows people to exchange one product for another.

Tweet-Enabled Treat Dispensers

The BEV Twitter vending machine trades hashtags for iced tea.

Interactive Digital Showrooms

Audi City provides customers with a virtual buying experience.

Augmented Reality Retailers

Airwalk created an invisible store in a real location that could only be seen through smartphones.

STEP 4: PUSH YOUR BOUNDARIES. Next, look for *less*-related ideas in places outside your particular challenge. Most great innovators seek inspiration from a broad range of sources. When I interviewed Mark Southern, the director of product innovation for Hilton Worldwide, he told me that one of the chain's biggest sources of inspiration was NASA. He said that they were inspired by NASA's use of interchangeable parts, a tactic used on the space shuttle to ensure that if an important part broke, it could be fixed with parts from something less critical. Using that tactic, Hilton standardized cutlery, dishes, appliances, and other parts across its 4,000 hotels. BMW's ConnectedDrive interface, meanwhile, was inspired by video gaming, and Reebok's new Shox shoes take their inspiration from the springs in a car. So look beyond your market, and take inspiration from some of these far-flung examples:

LESS-RELATED: IDEAS OUTSIDE OF YOUR MARKET

Fitting Room Simulators	**Self-Service Taverns**	**Storybook Photoshoots**
Try on clothes at home with Tobi.com's virtual dressing room.	The Thirsty Bear lets customers help themselves to beer.	MAC and Hello Kitty channeled *Alice in Wonderland*.
Impromptu Playgrounds	**FIFA Street Parties**	**Interactive Fitting Rooms**
Unexpected parks beautify your city while creating a place to play.	Adidas turned a parking lot into a bar for World Cup celebrants.	Try on any pair of shoes with the Converse sampler phone app.
Eco-Retro Vans That Expand	**Beauty Spa Buses**	**Doodle Art Creative Bars**
Retro VW camper goes green and turns into a campsite.	Clean Earth Design created a transportable, full-service spa.	London's Doodle Bar lets customers draw on everything, from floor to ceiling.

Clothing Subscriptions (Not a Store)	Interactive Electronic Mannequins	Fashion Food Trucks
Le Tote lets users rent full outfits for $49 per month.	TeamLabHanger created virtual mannequins that respond to gestures.	Henry Holland transformed an ice cream van into a fashion store.

By now, you've had a chance to check out quite a few different ideas. It's tempting to think "That's it!" and convince yourself that your next idea will be better informed. But there's another step. To ensure success, you need to train yourself to see different types of patterns and clusters.

STEP 5: COLLECT AND CLUSTER WHAT YOU FIND. You and your team need to be able to see and compare the most exciting and inspiring ideas. You might write up each idea on a Post-it and pin your collection on a board accompanied by photos or drawings. Or take a more traditional route and display your findings in PowerPoint, Keynote, or Excel. The key is to gather, display, and then look for patterns.

STEP 6: THROW AWAY YOUR FIRST CLUSTERS. The human mind is great at finding trends and patterns by creating shortcuts or by falling prey to stereotypes, schemas, and bias. We try to lighten our mental load by referencing what we've seen before and what we know works. To give you a sense of how strongly this tendency asserts itself, consider for a moment the painted lines in the middle of the road that keep us from colliding with another vehicle. We rely on similar guidelines in our day-to-day lives. Whether we recognize it or not, much of our day is conducted on autopilot. It's the reason we can walk up to a door and open it without thinking. We don't need to assess the door and figure out how it opens.

All of these automatic systems are essential, of course, but they're not so helpful if your goal is innovation. When this type of robotic thinking governs how you search for new ideas, it can hold you back. To break free, you often need to throw away your first idea.

For example, looking through the previous business examples, you might spot a cluster of similar ideas. And that might prompt you to attempt to sell something by mimicking one of these ideas. But there's a catch. If an idea has become popular enough to become a big business, it's probably pretty obvious. In fact, the concept is so obvious that it's almost generic. What can you do to reframe that idea? Or try something different? Using patterns, you can reshape or discover new opportunity.

STEP 7: USE THE SIX PATTERNS TO RE-CLUSTER YOUR INSIGHTS. If you look at the same group of ideas again and scan for other clusters and ideas, more-distinctive patterns will jump out:

- **Store within a Store** (reduction)—A store within a store may be the simplest concept. Inexpensive and quick to implement, this approach allows you to focus shopper attention on the novelty of your idea in comparison with the more familiar items in the larger retail space. The tactic explicitly carves out your products from everything else being sold alongside them—it is attention-focusing.

- **Billboard Store** (redirection)—The examples listed above include a "subway" supermarket that allows commuters to purchase products on the go and scannable product deliveries in which mobile devices allow instant purchase and delivery, and a billboard that is a library of downloadable books. These all attract attention. The billboard library repurposes the billboard for direct commerce. Dramatic and unexpected, it also has the benefit of being extremely scalable. If this week your pop-up billboard store takes off, you can expand with ten more billboards in the next month, and a hundred by the end of the year.

• **Virtual Reality Store** (acceleration)—The interactive window display, augmented reality sneaker shop, interactive fitting room, and interactive virtual mannequins all have something in common. Each accelerates an aspect of augmented reality to create something futuristic and exciting during a launch.

• **Nostalgic Escape** (cyclicality)—The storybook photo shoot, pop-up roller rinks, impromptu playground, and retro-designed fashion food truck examples all play the nostalgia card. By tapping into our past, they forge a deep emotional connection. Interestingly, none of these would be particularly expensive to create. They demonstrate the power of calculated design.

• **Anti-Store** (divergence)—Some businesses succeed because they challenge our mainstream beliefs by consciously removing service, choice, and tradition. Because they break so violently with our expectations, a certain consumer segment often finds them appealing. Consider the self-serve alcohol bar (removing service), the clothing subscription (removing choices), and the pedal-powered cinema (removing the movie tradition of passively sitting). Each draws energy from dramatically challenging our expectations.

• **Grouped Experience** (convergence)—The pop-up FIFA party, pop-up dinner party, and pop-up party bus all show the immense power of creating a mass, onetime event. They are convergence points for other ideas and events already grabbing attention. They capitalize on being the ideal place to attract a confluence of surrounding ideas.

• **Double Business** (convergence)—Many of these ideas are twice as likely to succeed because they pack multiple businesses into one destination. There's the art gallery/fashion shop, coffee shop/pop-up bank, and movie-theater/couture shop. These cross-over, double-purpose shops give people more reasons to check them out, and they provide something unusual to talk about, making it far more likely they'll be noticed.

• **Final Challenge**—Now it's time to destroy. Throw away your first concept, pick one of the above clusters, and spend some time thinking about your business. In all likelihood, your second iteration will take advantage of new ideas and be more exciting and more focused.

Ultimately, you're looking for a cluster. Taking that path will help you brainstorm ideas, prototype new concepts, and come up with an insight that's more likely to be successful because it doesn't rely on gut instinct. Rather, it will leverage the power of an underlying pattern.

Chapter 12

LOOKING AT INDIVIDUAL INDUSTRIES

To help people make meaningful change, I often find that it's
enough to paint them a picture of what *could* be. But I also need
to point out the risk of inaction. In trying to imagine how the
world will evolve, people are always energized about the *distant* future, playfully dreaming of what's possible in a decade or more. But
when it comes to making near-term business decisions, they tend
to stop looking forward. There is comfort in assuming that things
won't change too much, whether in our jobs, relationships, or anywhere else. Even if we *can* foresee certain aspects of our industry's
future, it's likely we'll underestimate the scope of change.

To clarify the pace of transformation, it helps to look backward.
Let's contrast, for example, the consumer experience of movie-
going in 2000 versus 2010.

Consider the movie industry. If you were working at Warner
Brothers in 2010, you would have wanted to know about the near-
term future of big-screen entertainment. You would have noticed
that people were streaming movies online, but you might have mistakenly dismissed the growth of online downloading because traditional movies screened in theaters were still setting records. The
box office would have been your status quo. When it came to the *far*
distant future, you could have easily daydreamed about advanced
3D, heightened interactivity, virtual reality, and personalization.
But those ideas would have seemed so far off that it would have

been tough to convince others to make urgent changes to prepare. Plus, the then-current, theater-centric movie business model would have appeared to be still working.

So how might you have prepared your organization for the future? A starting point would have been to study the change that had already happened. You might have rewound to the year 2000 and imagined a night out with friends. To select a movie in that first year of the new millennium, you likely would have scoured your pile of newspapers to find the latest flicks. Perhaps you would have settled on *X-Men*, but when you realized that your paper was a few days old, you would have needed to verify the show times. By telephone! If you happened to have a cell phone, that wouldn't have helped. In the year 2000, few smartphones existed, and the options for online movie show times were limited. You literally would have had to dial the theater's number, patiently listen to all the announcements before confirming your movie time, and then hang up to call your friends. Many probably wouldn't even have mobile phones, so you might have had to leave messages on their answering machines. Finally, you would have had to hop into your car and head to the theater. Since this was way before the popularization of GPS, you would have had to know where you were going, and, strange as it sounds, back then, few people regularly used printed maps. When you did finally arrive, you might have learned to your dismay that the movie was sold out. You would have then needed a backup plan, which might have involved visiting the closest mall to shop for sneakers and grab a bite to eat.

In the following decade, everything about that night out changed.

In 2010, if you wanted to see a movie with those same friends, you might have selected *The Social Network*, about the founders of Facebook. You might have decided to save some bucks by streaming the movie at home, but if you wanted to meet your friends IRL ("In Real Life"), you could have pinged them via e-mail, sent a text, or used Facebook itself to communicate. While you waited for their reply, you might have picked up your smartphone and done some pre-movie research. For example, you might have used your favorite movie app to review *The Social Network* trailer and to check crowd-sourced ratings. (And by the time you'd scanned your preview, your friends might have pinged you back with a happy face emoticon.) You'd then have the option of buying advance tickets, and you could use GPS to find the theater. If you'd decided to go the advance buying route, you would have arrived with a guaranteed ticket, with no need to wait in line or risk getting stuck with a crappy seat. You could have then put those extra minutes to good use—for example, by tracking down the closest Starbucks or places to shop. All from your smartphone.

Perhaps the biggest change in that period was that by 2010, you might have skipped the movie altogether. By 2010, viewers' time was increasingly dominated by Internet videos, web browsing, and video games. Teenagers had shifted to spending far more time surfing the Internet than viewing traditional television. Online videos of all shapes and sizes had exploded, and millions of websites had begun catering to every niche of the moviegoing public. The video game industry rapidly shot past box office sales. For comparison, in 2000 the hit movie *X-Men* earned $54 million on its opening weekend, and roughly $300 million total. In 2014, the hit video game *Grand Theft Auto V* earned an astounding $800 million in its first day of sales and $1 billion in three days—an entertainment record that makes *X-Men*'s total seem puny.[1]

The point is that comparing 2000 to 2010 makes it easier to anticipate the pace of change. Looking back a mere ten years, it now seems prehistoric to find a movie listing in a newspaper or to search

---

1   Erik Kain, "'Grand Theft Auto V' Crosses $1B in Sales, Biggest Entertainment Launch in History," *Forbes*, September 20, 2013, http://www.forbes.com/sites/erik kain/2013/09/20/grand-theft-auto-v-crosses-1b-in-sales-biggest-entertainment -launch-in-history.

for directions on a printed map. And not only that—the movie-going experience itself has been transformed in many other ways. Indeed, in a simple night at the movies, we can see a dozen industries destroyed, transformed, and created. The era of traditional movies, landline phones, not-so-smart cell phones, phone books, print newspapers, and paper maps has been eclipsed by smartphones, messaging, crowd-sourced reviews, online shopping, and social video games.

In 2011, Warner Brothers strategists began connecting the dots by purchasing the movie-rating site Rotten Tomatoes and the movie app Flickster. These acquisitions plugged Warner Brothers into the evolving movie-choosing experience, and, more important, they gave the company a digital platform with superior long-term possibilities. As owners of the top movie app and rating site, the company is ideally positioned to launch new digital products, shape movie decisions, and—as some speculate—have a shot one day at rivaling Netflix. While Warner Brothers has adapted far faster than many of its competitors, it could have been more prescient. Had the studio undertaken the above exercise of understanding the pace of change, it might have had a digital platform years earlier, saving millions and beating Netflix, Google Play, and Apple to seize control of the digital download marketplace.

One clear takeaway here is that you're more likely to convince yourself and others of the dramatic pace of change when you think holistically about major shifts in your customer's experience. Internalizing the pace of change is key because it will push you to make predictions that aren't anchored in the status quo and it will imbue your plan with a sense of urgency.

KEY INDUSTRIES TO TRACK

For a trend hunter, paying attention to the next few years is critical because it can spark extraordinary opportunity. However, most people spend too much time studying the current state of their industry without thinking more broadly about their future customer. As the moviegoing experience shows, to unlock bigger opportunities, it is important to think comprehensively about potential major changes to your customer's life three, five, and even ten years into the future. One powerful way to internalize behavioral shifts is by studying multiple markets.

For example, taking note of a hot retro 1980s-style dress can spur you to think about cyclical opportunities far afield from fashion. Seeing the dress might influence you to pay attention to a related trend—for instance, how 1980s video game fashion has been creeping into social media. Then you might, by chance, stumble on a new vintage-style beer ad and suddenly become enthusiastic about what your company can do to leverage nostalgia focused on the same era.

"Those who don't know history are destined to repeat it," wrote the Irish philosopher and statesman Edmund Burke. We study history in school and college for many reasons, not the least of which is that it helps us avoid repeating tired old plans and policies that will no longer work. The section below will prime you on the pace of change in key industries by looking at the products and services historically associated with that industry. Each of these industries serves markets that are complex, so keep in mind that my summaries are, of necessity, oversimplified. They're merely designed to illustrate important changes that Trend Hunter has been tracking based on our work with top-tier innovators in each market.

Fashion

Fashion has long been the canary in the coal mine for spotting nascent consumer trends. The industry moves fast, the players are competitive, and contemporary culture greatly influences what works and what doesn't.

Fashion is fascinating because it's largely unbounded by barriers to entry. It may surprise you, but fashion designers don't benefit from copyright protection because apparel is considered a "staple" like food, beverages, and household products. To be protectable, a design must qualify as a sculpture, pictorial, or copy-written graphic. This essentially leaves designers free to copy one another's work (the exception is that fashion brands can protect their trade-marked logos, which explains in part why so many high-end labels, such as Louis Vuitton or Chanel, adorn their products with their corporate logos). What's amazing is that this general lack of legal design protection has unleashed unbridled creativity and fast-paced evolution.

THEN Around the turn of the twenty-first century, the fashion market was competitive, but styles were far more consistent. Giant production runs, big ad campaigns, and big media greatly reduced variety. This general sameness across the industry wasn't surprising. A few decades ago, we all watched the same prime-time television shows, read the same magazines, and generally held to a more consistent view of popular culture. Teenagers took their style cues from the same handful of celebrities. Thanks to the Internet, those days are long gone. Everything is hyper-individualized, from role models to niche communities to, ultimately, our preferences. Designers can no longer create just one perfect line, prop it up with a massive ad campaign, stick it in a catalogue, and expect it to sell throughout the next season.

NOW Fashion has been heavily influenced by divergence and the desire for personalization. As we have seen, fast-fashion retailers such as Zara and H&M have enjoyed tremendous success by offering tens of thousands of different items. Their approach has shattered the conventional retailer wisdom that offerings should be minimized to benefit economies of scale and inventory management. Some retailers have taken the desire for personalization even further by allowing users to customize their own dresses or suits online. Fashion sites such as Polyvore enable enthusiasts to piece together their own collections and outfits, which are then either adored or criticized by the crowd. With this increased control over one's fashion identity has come the rise of the "fashionista" and popular communities such as LOOKBOOK, where millions of fashion lovers share their daily look and gain inspiration from real people around the globe. Movie and TV celebrities are losing their central position as fashion role models.

This leads to a lesson that's key to innovators and entrepreneurs: Fashion extends beyond clothing.

At first, you may think that fashion is unrelated to your business. Over the last decade, my colleagues and I at Trend Hunter have found that even our most technical clients now care about subtle changes in style and preference. *Everyone* cares about aesthetics. It's clear, for example, that the tech giant Samsung aspires to make a more fashionable smartphone than Apple. Similarly, LG Electronics logically wants an interconnected fridge that's more stylish. And even Intel needs to anticipate what the fashion will be for wireless devices in the future.

LOOKING FORWARD Convergence with technology will continue to grow within the fashion industry, resulting in everything from wearable technology to interactive changing rooms that use augmented reality to help the customer visualize different outfits in different settings. Innovators outside the industry will increasingly blend their products with fashion. For example, GM was one of the first automakers to use fashion shows to introduce its cars. And since 2005, Samsung has been working to discover and recruit up-and-coming Korean fashion designers—an effort that has enabled the company to advance the style of its technology that has proven to be essential in its battle against rival technology makers such as Apple.

Pattern-Based Opportunities

Divergence: Today, only a few companies are truly capable of fast fashion and personalization, but as others adapt, fashion will explode with choice and extreme customization. Why buy your shoes at the mall when you can learn what shoe best fits your foot and then order the exact color combinations and materials that suit your preference? In apparel, this type of personalization is an intuitive trend, but fashion's lead will influence many other markets to incorporate customization.

Convergence: The convergence of design, technology, new materials, and shopping trends will spark many new opportunities in what we wear. Expect convergence in wearable technology, 3D printed fashion, augmented-reality changing rooms, tech-enabled sporting apparel, and more advanced materials.

Redirection: As technology enables every company to become faster at fashion, the most enduring way to create longer-term value will be through the power of a brand and its purpose. Smarter use of social media and experiential branding will enable companies to redirect brands to subcultures, values, and social causes.

Cyclicality: Fashion will, of course, always be subject to retro trend and other cyclical shifts. Pay attention to fashion and you will find within it other cultural shifts that apply to your industry.

Technology

Every decade or so, there is a rotation of technology leaders. Consider a simple and focused industry such as computer hard drive manufacturers. In 1980, the market for 14-inch drives was dominated by Control Data, IBM, and Memorex. Yet all three were rendered obsolete just four years later by firms pioneering the 8-inch drive, led by Shugart. The top three in the 8-inch market were displaced just four years after that by leaders in the 6.25-inch market, topped by Seagate. Only one of those competitors—Connor—remained at the top five years later when 3.5-inch drives were all the rage. And within two years, a company called Prairetek surpassed them all to lead the 2.5-inch market. From the outside, the evolution toward smaller drives seemed inevitable. Yet somehow, the leaders failed to adapt.

THEN Back in 2000, technology was thought of as one big industry with unlimited promise. Computer makers, cell phone makers, software developers, and dot-com entrepreneurs were often grouped under the same nerdy and somewhat cloudy umbrella, and "geeks" were thought to be set to rule the world. Of course, that bubble burst in 2001. Back then, consumer excitement was heavily influenced by hardware and technical specifications. People wanted a faster processor, more memory, better resolution, and as many features as possible.

NOW Today, it's abundantly clear that technology is a massive part of everyone's life and nearly every company's success. There are countless opportunities for technology convergence—and, in particular, a myriad of ways to bring mobile capabilities into industries that have resisted change. Faster computers generating massive quantities of information—so-called "big data"—are making possible more-informed corporate strategy. Advanced e-commerce techniques and social media–based targeting are making advertising decisions more precise and predictive. Hardware is moving to the background with an increased focus on user experience, design, and software. Smart companies are hiring and paying attention to millennials who, by coming of age in a digital world, have a unique advantage.

We've seen how quickly the look and feel of machines have evolved—from desktop PCs to laptops to smartphones to tablets. In each of these categories, technical specifications and processing power once dominated our interest, but people no longer crave a faster phone. Design, software, and the larger "ecosystem" of apps are what excite people today. As nearly all smartphones evolve into thin, light, and fast devices, what distinguishes one from another is quite simply what you can do with it.

LOOKING FORWARD So what's next? We're entering the age of wearable and embedded technologies. In the far-distant future, like it or not, millions will use technology to boost their vision and senses and gain nearly instant omnipresent access to information, memories, and entertainment.

Dramatic? Perhaps. But consider the following: The first bionic eyes were implanted in 2002, thought-controlled videos games were being experimented with in 2010, and by 2013, Google had squeezed the power of a computer into a pair of glasses. Widespread tech integration will not be a question of "if" but "when."

No, it won't all be rosy. If you want to explore the potential downside of pervasive emerging technology, check out the third episode of *Black Mirror*, a British television series that imagines the future impact of certain technologies. In that episode of *Black Mirror*, called "The Entire History of You," humankind has become overly reliant on an Internet-connected memory bank implanted behind the ear. People can recall memories, reexperience their past, and access near-unlimited information. Though it sounds cool, what might it mean for their relationships? The episode features a couple who are stuck like an old record in a bad groove—reliving their worst arguments and struggles. Imagine always being able to recall your partner's worst words or having the ability to relive those scenes that sparked anger and jealousy. That can't be good for a relationship.

Still, in exchange for the bad there will be an awful lot happening that is exciting and helpful. Future generations will be shaped by more-personalized products and experiences because technology has made it possible to quickly generate short-run productions and custom-made goods. You'll be 3D printing designs just for you, living longer thanks to bioengineering, and using products that incorporate never-dreamed-of-before advanced materials. The companies you love will be leveraging data to create experiences and products that cater to your needs. Advertisements will be personalized, and entertainment will engage more senses.

There will be laggards, of course—companies that fail to use social media, cling to outdated web browsers, and try to get by with cumbersome, slow computers. Over time, they'll be crushed by the legions of hungry, crowd-sourcing, crowd-filtering companies that are structured for disruption. Ask yourself some tough questions: What rival companies are eyeing *your* market? What start-ups or venture capitalists are moving in on *your* industry? Ten years from now, what will a company in your industry need to look like to dominate or just to survive?

Pattern-Based Opportunities

Reduction: Technology has leveled the playing field, spawning platforms that empower individual entrepreneurs. Some of these platforms include eBay, Fiverr, Kickstarter, and the app marketplaces of Google, Apple, and Amazon. All of these sites and functionalities permit consumers to elegantly solve a need.

Acceleration: New technologies allow innovative companies to rethink what consumers truly like, and they make it far easier to create more-powerful experiences. Innovations in wearable technology, virtual reality, and social media will help entrepreneurs re-engineer their business.

Divergence: Tomorrow's products and services will be far more crafted and targeted, thanks to technology that enables better personalization in both the digital and real worlds. From customized product design to 3D printed objects, a whole new way of meeting people's individual needs is emerging.

Retail

How we shop for goods is rapidly changing, and the impact spans nearly all categories. To better understand the massive transformation under way in retail, it's essential to explore how we jumped from dreary beige shopping malls to social-media-empowered shopping and augmented-reality changing rooms.

THEN In the late 1990s, retail stores were where we went to buy clothes, staples, and gadgets. Big-box stores dominated, competing on selection and price. Then came e-commerce and the ultimate battle for price and selection. Storefronts were suddenly viewed as antiquated and dismissed as mere "brick and mortar." Following the bandwagon, many brands mistakenly poured too much energy into their websites.

But then something unexpected happened. The dot-com bubble burst, stinging those who'd overinvested online and ushering in a new conservatism.

More rough waters lay ahead. In 2007, the economy collapsed, sending some of the largest retailers into bankruptcy, including Circuit City, Linens 'n Things, KB Toys, Borders Books, Ritz Cameras, and Eddie Bauer. Countless more chains were forced to restructure. Many retailers held back on store renovations, clinging to basic and simplified designs. Although a few noteworthy retailers pioneered new models, it was a decade marked by limited retail innovation.

At the same time, social media began taking over the marketing conversation, and brands realized that each individual consumer was suddenly capable of broadcasting store experiences—good or bad. It was both a massive opportunity and a public relations nightmare.

NOW Companies have been urgently upgrading their retail store layouts, technology, and branding. They seek to emulate the "darlings"—companies such as Starbucks, Urban Outfitters, Lululemon, Apple, and Victoria's Secret, which have excelled at designing physical store experiences and surfed through the downturns. Shops have remodeled to heighten the brand experience, and large retailers have started creating pop-up shops and store-within-a-store experiences. Many malls have upgraded their food courts and heightened aesthetics to enhance the feel of a mall as a destination rather than just a place to shop. Brands, meanwhile, have started using mobile marketing and social media to connect with customers in the store.

LOOKING FORWARD In the next decade, retailers will spend more time and money investing in retail technology and physical stores as they strive to create deep cultural experiences with their niche customers. Many industry leaders view that approach as the only defense against the onslaught of e-commerce. They see hope in a more holistic convergence pattern. For example, your future trip to the grocery store is likely to feature increased digital integration, menu inspiration catered to your specific interests, and in-store experiences (for example, interaction with visiting chefs and nutrition experts) that will boost your interest in healthy eating and appreciation of food as a celebratory meal. You'll probably try more, buy more, and enjoy your life more because of how technology changes your daily experience with food.

Pattern-Based Opportunities

Convergence: For many companies, physical stores, marketing programs, and e-commerce sites have started to combine. In the near future, different types of convergence will result in countless opportunities, including social media–empowered shopping, hybrid stores, and augmented reality (digital changing rooms and virtual experiences).

Reduction: Expect an ongoing simplification of shopping based on people's desire for that which is simple or catered. This trend will fuel subscription businesses, non-monetary payment (pay with a tweet or barter), niche vending, delayed delivery (the store as a place to order, versus online), and focused store concepts.

Divergence: With the big-box, online shopping, and economies-of-scale trends of the past decade pushing us toward a gray retail landscape of giant bland shops, there's a clear need for something unique. This will fuel our appetite for focused themes, store-within-a-store convenience, pop-up shops, extreme levels of service, personalization, and "shoppertainment," meaning in-store experiences created to delight shoppers.

Broadcast and Media

The Internet and mobile technology have shifted the balance of media power from a few major broadcasters to millions of individual content producers. Broadcasters have launched major initiatives to change, knowing that they must "adapt or die," but the bigger shifts to come are related to corporations. Nearly all corporations have become media companies, publishing in social media at the very least and in their own blogs and videos at the very best. As ad dollars are increasingly diverted to social media platforms, the media landscape will change even further.

THEN Back in the 1990s, power was concentrated. A few giant broadcasters controlled the airwaves, a handful of networks dominated television, and several newspaper chains controlled the nation's newspapers. Creating quality content—newscasts, TV and radio dramas, and magazine and newspaper articles—was expensive. Advertising on the best shows or in the best publications often meant committing the majority of a corporation's marketing budget—millions of dollars a year.

NOW Today, that entire system can be bypassed. Companies and individuals can gain phenomenal traction with a viral video or compelling story. The world has shifted from one-to-many to many-to-many, which is already impacting our lives, our individual styles, our product choices, and our sense of belonging.

This shift has inflicted brutal pain on broadcasters, print magazines, and traditional print newspapers, many of which have been forced to downsize or declare bankruptcy. Result: Old-school media is reviewing its rigid commitment to story lengths, video formats, and salary levels that have proven out of touch with the new reality.

Imagine you work at a newspaper, magazine, or television broadcaster in a medium-sized city. In the past, these traditional media outlets might have paid several thousand dollars for a story. Now millions of bloggers can beat those same companies to the punch with faster news for just a few dollars a story. If you worked in the industry, your first move might be to compete with bloggers through rigorous journalism. Unfortunately, today people are conditioned to go to their favorite website for breaking news. They are creatures of habit rather than judges of journalistic quality. And they value speed.

LOOKING FORWARD Television broadcasters will need to protect themselves from streaming services and online media by developing more-immersive experiences, such as virtual reality (which will change everything about how we experience the world), 3D, interactive television, or the ability to allow viewers to choose their own adventure. Overwhelmed by ad-free Internet radio and listeners who opt to stream music to their cars using their phones, radio broadcasters will need to focus on their local stronghold to monetize their services. Newspapers belatedly made the shift to online—in most cases, not soon enough to prevent their advertisers from fleeing. To survive, remaining newspapers will need to completely restructure. Some will turn to local expertise, others will downsize dramatically, and a few will make the leap to new forms of media.

Individuals will continue to become more important publishers of stories, podcasts, and videos. With so many people participating, curators and aggregators will play a more important role. For example, people are already increasingly more likely to discover news stories through a Facebook feed than through a visit to their favorite news site.

Technology will increasingly transform how we experience media, through gaming, interactivity, virtual reality, holograms, personalization, 3D, and the integration of social networks. Instead of playing a video game or watching a movie, imagine choosing your own 3D, adventure-style movie that has been personalized to your preferences and stars you and your friends. Emerging media technology is particularly appealing to big publishers because they believe that it may prove more immune to piracy and that the barriers to entry are higher.

Finally, the most interesting and powerful force shaping media, as we've discussed, is that every company in the world is becoming a publisher and broadcaster. In the early years of social media, companies were connecting with their customers through Twitter and Facebook, but in a market in which people increasingly skip past ads, content is the most influential way to connect. Compelling stories are one of the best possible advertisements, and that's why companies will become more interested in the curation and development of their own content. And it's why, ironically, some of what made media giants great—superior broadcast talent, great writers, and engaging radio hosts—will allow them to reemerge as a potent force. Why advertise in the media when you can *own* the media? Brands such as Red Bull, Diesel, and Dove have already pioneered this transition, creating powerful videos as early as 2006 that went viral. Red Bull Media House was founded in 2007. The energy drink maker describes it as a "multiplatform media company with a focus on sports, culture, and lifestyle" that offers "a wide range of premium media products and compelling content across media channels as diverse as TV, mobile, digital, audio, and print."

Pattern-Based Opportunities

Convergence: The next decade will see an explosion of media convergence, as new technologies combine with increased competition from content producers. Expect more brands participating in media production (instead of spending money on advertising). Also, expect more interactive experiences (such as augmented reality, virtual reality, and choosing your own adventure), integration of web and television, convergence of video gaming and television, and shoppable entertainment.

Divergence: To stand out in a media-cluttered world, companies large and small will need to create something truly divergent or personalized, which will mean personalized content, personalized ads, and unexpected experiences. Live broadcasters will be upping the ante with new technologies and more-immersive live experience, particularly in sports with augmented reality, live stats, integrated social feeds (for example, watching your friends' reaction as you watch), and three-dimensionality.

Reduction: Future opportunities in broadcasting will be about simplification and finding business models unencumbered by legacy cost structures.

Food

How we eat and shop for food is evolving, fueled by a greater awareness of ingredients, health, wellness, Internet foodie culture, and the generational shift of boomers aging and being more conscious of how their choices influence their health.

THEN Kellogg's Cornflakes, Kraft Mac and Cheese, Spam, Doritos, and Heinz ketchup are just a few examples of popular packaged goods that dominated the shelves and dinner tables of American homes for decades. These iconic brands endured recessions and became engrained in popular culture. Shopping for food historically involved a weekly trip to the big neighborhood grocery store to purchase these and other highly branded and advertised consumer packaged goods. Fresh fruits and vegetables were rarely a large portion of the menu.

NOW Eating habits and shopping for food are being reshaped by our growing concerns about health and food sourcing and by a renewed desire to turn meals with friends or family into celebrations. Pack-

LOOKING AT INDIVIDUAL INDUSTRIES / 217

aged foods are facing ever-greater scrutiny. People everywhere are increasingly concerned about preservatives, fat, sugar, and salt (and even gluten and dairy), fueled by documentaries, media attention, and celebrities such as Jamie Oliver and Michelle Obama taking a stand against the obesity epidemic in America. Nutrition and taste are winning ground against packaged, unhealthy options.

Popular documentaries about fast food, overfishing, and genetic modification of foods have also heightened consumer interest in re-evaluating food choices. The trend is toward health and wellness, and that means natural products, wellness-based eating, alternative diets, and buying locally from trusted farmers. Eyeing customers' new priorities, some companies have cut their portion sizes, reduced the amount of "bad" ingredients, or created healthier substitutes—see, for example, Burger King's "Satisfries," which boast 40 percent less fat than their "normal" fries.

Meanwhile, a glamorized foodie culture has emerged, rife with celebrity chefs and a plethora of televised cooking competitions. The Internet has popularized food blogging and the social media phenomenon of photographing one's meals in restaurants and at home. This celebration of food sparks interest in specialty dishes and foods, mom-and-pop brands, and better eating habits. People are subscribing in huge numbers to cheese clubs, wine clubs, and cooking kits for gourmet meals. There are even subscriptions for personalized food plans, and consumers can purchase custom granola bars and supplements that are just right for them.

LOOKING FORWARD In the expanding markets for food, convergence is the essential pattern to exploit. The winners will tap into the booming convergence of health, sourcing, and experience. Many of the largest, most powerful brands will be pressured to quickly adapt, adjusting their ingredients and sourcing. But just as the early computer giants failed to adapt to the personal computer revolution or see the potential of the Internet, most consumer packaged-goods companies will struggle. Quite simply, their bias is toward protecting their strong brand equity. They farm. A client at one of the most powerful consumer packaged-goods companies recently told me that her brand is super at what she called "productionizing and optimizing a product," but weak at finding the "right" new products and at diverging from traditional thinking.

Of course, shopping for food will also be heavily influenced by the growth of online shopping. In addition to signing up for food subscriptions, people will be increasingly drawn to online retailers, which will offer the same fresh food conveniently delivered at a lower price. The online food industry will be further fueled by smart-home technology that will result in your having an Internet-connected kitchen, bringing recipes, coaching, digital inventory management, and grocery delivery. Food lovers will find it easier to order the ingredients included in the recipes they've seen on their favorite blogs and cooking shows. With one click, they'll be able to get all the ingredients and directions needed to emulate their favorite Michelin star chef or food blogger.

Pattern-Based Opportunities

Reduction: Simplification will continue to be a compelling pattern in the food industry. Expect to see explosive experimentation with simplicity and more single-food pop-ups, food trucks, and unique shops, such as those that only sell juice, yogurt, cupcakes, chocolate, and so on. The Internet will enable more subscription services for that single treat or food kit—from cheese to chocolate to wine. Also, consumers will see "portioned delight" bite-sized versions of higher-calorie fare, such as cupcakes, burgers, and so on.

Cyclicality: We've already witnessed how the fashion industry's exploitation of '60s, '70s, and '80s nostalgia has been a commercial hit. The same trend will continue in food with the resurgence of classics such as cheese sandwiches.

Convergence: Many companies will partner with other market players in creative co-branding efforts and forge links to other businesses through the growth of wellness programs.

Entrepreneurship

Entrepreneurial aspirations are increasing and upending the traditional business landscape. In small business, the number of start-ups and new players entering the game has soared. In big corporations, entrepreneurial thinking is becoming the tool of choice for attacking new market opportunities and heightening an organization's ability to adapt. To better understand what's happening, it's worth reflecting on this major transition.

THEN When baby boomers first entered the job market in the late 1960s and 1970s, many felt heavy pressure from their war-era parents to secure solid, dependable jobs and provide for their families. During that era, many American blue-chip companies were expanding steadily, and a Fortune 500 job was a badge of honor, representing stability and status.

NOW Today, entrepreneurial aspirations have replaced the pursuit of blue-chip stability. Between 2004 and 2014, the number of people searching for "blue chip" on Google dropped in half, while searches for "entrepreneur" leaped by 50 percent. Government statistics show a huge rise in the number of men and women launching small businesses. A Darwinian process is under way. Increasingly, people want to be part of something that grows and adapts—whether it's a start-up, a small company, or a large company that recognizes the need to offer many of the same attributes of smaller, more-nimble firms.

Quite simply, organizations need to be better equipped to adapt, much like a start-up. Mass production and economies of scale have lost their central position. Meanwhile, multiple demographic shifts are fueling entrepreneurship, including the increasing numbers of millennial workers, women in the workforce, and "work till they drop" baby boomers.

Millennial workers have been smacked hard with the highest post-school unemployment rates in decades. Highly creative and intensely motivated to pursue fulfilling work and life choices, this generation may possibly come to be defined by its entrepreneurial bent. Millennials have come of age in a period in which multiple online communities have facilitated hobby businesses, including Etsy, Fiverr, eBay, and Kickstarter. Twenty-somethings and thirty-somethings view entrepreneurial ambitions as normal, and they are comfortable with earning their livelihood from multiple sources while they experiment with potential ventures.

Women entrepreneurs now make up one of the largest segments of new business owners. Gender equality has gained prominence, and today, far more women find themselves in positions of power (perhaps most visibly, Facebook's Sheryl Sandberg and Yahoo's Marissa Mayer). Countless online publications and communities exist to inspire women to pursue their ambitions. Female bloggers—from twenty-somethings (such as Elise Andrew of "I Love F**king Science") to mommy bloggers—are often more successful than their male counterparts.

Boomers, meanwhile, are teaching us that today, sixty is the new fifty. Boomers are active, athletic, and hardworking, eagerly funding start-ups and embracing hobby businesses and passion projects. Interestingly, they team extraordinarily well with millennials. Research shows that boomers, with their broad experience, robust financial resources, and rich talent network, are likely to be more successful in starting small businesses or start-ups than any other demographic.

LOOKING FORWARD The removal of barriers to entry will continue to catalyze change. Technology makes it far simpler to identify market needs, prototype products, access funding, secure partners, create brand presence, and connect with customers. The urgent message for larger companies is that to survive, they need to become more entrepreneurial. But the good news is that workers have never been better equipped to make such a transition. The same resources that make it easy to launch a new venture can be used to experiment with new products and services. Entrepreneurs, take note: No longer do you need to make a big investment and take the full leap. Online tools and platforms and the ability to find kindred support among fellow part-timers make it possible to moonlight and experiment.

Pattern-Based Opportunities

Reduction: With so many platforms for selling and bartering one's services, it has never been easier to start a simple business that solves a single problem, which means that the future will be filled with more passion-based businesses and ultra-niche services.

Cyclicality: Since so much entrepreneurial activity is occurring within the boomer demographic, there are predictable opportunities in wellness—but also in all the activities a boomer might become involved with, including hobby businesses.

Redirection: The start-ups and new ventures that stand out will be those that create a deeper connection—for example, tourism with a purpose and businesses with an embedded social good. Consumers will respond not just to the product but to an authentic mission.

QUICK THOUGHTS ON A FEW ADDITIONAL INDUSTRIES

Beyond the handful of major industries that you should regularly keep tabs on, there may be others that have surprising relevance to your market or personal passions. The following examples are especially ripe for cross-pollination and idea-sowing:

AUTO The auto industry was one of the first to discard the farming paradigm in favor of hunting. After the 2008 financial crash, American automakers were forced to hunt for ways to satisfy dramatic shifts in consumer preference. There was also a new player on the scene. Tesla dramatically showed how investment in superior engineering, new technology, and a fresh business model can disrupt even the most investment-heavy industry. Today, most auto manufacturers are experimenting with hybrid technology, hydrogen fuel cells, and electric power. Some are even experimenting with "autonomous driving," which refers to a technology that allows cars to anticipate dangers and shuttle passengers around town on autopilot. Meanwhile, car design is increasingly ruled by fashion. Since our "wheels" express our personality, style, and status, car shoppers will continue to see new shapes, eye-catching concepts, and retro designs that tap into our love of bygone eras and classic car brands. (Often, new cars are crafted with such subtlety that we don't always recognize they're retro.) Opportunities in this segment include mobile device integration, streaming connectivity, driverless cars and autonomous safety, budget electric vehicles, and fashion and design.

FINANCE Finance is a counterintuitive place to study innovation. People often mistakenly think of finance as an industry overwhelmed by gray-suit thinking. But as a trend-spotter who got his start in banking, I admire the finance industry's calculated approach to diversification, its high-risk ideas, and its willingness to destroy what's worked in the past. What I *don't* admire are the bad actors who game the system, breaking trust with their clients and the public. Financial experts are, typically, among the most attuned to cyclical patterns. Sound investment strategies are often based on divergent thinking, and a keen understanding of finance can frequently be converged with your product to create a more lucrative business model. Take the freemium business model that is used with many video game products. (In that model, a core product is given away for free to a large group of users, and premium products are subsequently sold to a smaller fraction of the larger user base.) You might be surprised to learn that the model is based on the way people make short-term financial decisions. Similarly, the success of the subscription model is rooted in our tendency to make financial decisions cautiously: We'll say yes to the first month, and we'll delay saying no because we've already made our past decision. Finally, "portfolio management" (the idea that a product line is more likely to be successful if it combines assets with different risk characteristics) can be used to explain why a company might want to push a more aggressive innovation into its offering. Opportunities include social banking, crowd lending, gamified investing, investments in spreading financial literacy, automated and optimized investing, and financial product convergence.

HEALTH CARE With boomers aging, niche diets all the rage, and nutrition concerns on the rise, health and wellness will become a chief concern over the next few decades. There will be many opportunities for converging health and wellness. Pharmaceutical companies are getting far more involved in preventative health, and hospitals are offering amenities and services normally seen in the hospitality industry. Fitness is on the cusp of being fully integrated with technology, foretelling a boom in health and fitness apps and services (don't just think of "wearables" such as fitness wristwatches or wired clothing that monitor heart rate, but also video games that promote physical and mental wellness and that offer multidimensional experiences). As more boomers retire, we'll see a surge in products that promote longevity, brain health, and wellness. Opportunities include preventative health and wellness, digital monitoring, social fitness, and destination procedures.

ECO Environmental awareness has grown slowly in America—as compared to, say, Germany, which adopted widespread packaging and recycling laws as early as 1991. But by the early 2000s, Americans began acquiring eco-friendly products for their homes, partly as symbols of luxury. Today, environmentalism is close to becoming mainstream in America and many other Western nations. Still, we live in a time when environmental issues are often debated, and scientific "facts" differ depending on who is articulating them. Sadly, some experts think that it will take a disaster of some sort—the environmental version of a market meltdown—to inspire substantive change. Whatever the impetus, the world needs to awaken its inner hunter when it comes to environmental progress. Those who sit on the sidelines are taking the greatest risk. The next eco-catastrophe could create a divergent backlash against companies that have resisted integrating eco features into their offerings. Opportunities include recycled goods, cradle-to-grave products (ones made with their end state in mind), reduced carbon footprinting, sustainable packaging, gamified efficiency, reduced consumption, and products that embed social good.

LUXURY The rich continue to get richer, with income inequality arguably wider than the years before the Great Depression. This will continue to fuel demand for ridiculously expensive luxury goods, such as bigger yachts and quarter-million-dollar cars. But this trend has also bred growing resentment. Many luxury goods run the risk of appearing ostentatious, particularly if the widening gap between rich and poor isn't addressed before the next inevitable downward economic cycle. New luxury products will likely be less about status and more about personalization, which, like the ultra-luxury category, is also divergent, but carries less potential backlash. Opportunities include super luxury (for the growing 1 percent), extreme customization, and luxury eco or socially responsible products.

EDUCATION Today's classrooms cry out for radical technology reform. The "reverse" knowledge gap has never been wider between students and teachers. Kids are remarkably adept at exploiting the latest apps, websites, and programming languages, while teachers lag far behind. When any fact or date can be instantly referenced on a mobile phone, should we care if our children can recite them from memory? Or is it more important for them to be able to quickly prototype a new idea on a tablet and print it out on a 3D printer? Both university and K–12 education demand a complete technology overhaul and a deeper integration of the core principles of entrepreneurship and innovation. But there's a huge underlying problem. Education is one of the most traditional "farming" industries. At most institutions, innovation in educational methods is more or less stagnant, and money is increasingly being spent on fancy dorms, giant athletic centers, and shiny research facilities rather than on actual education methods. Four years of college in the United States can cost a staggering quarter-million dollars or more. Perhaps not surprisingly, college enrollment declined in the United States in 2012 for the first time in decades, and online courses threaten to draw away millions of students. New firms such as 2U, edX, and Coursera are partnering with traditional universities such as UC Berkeley, Harvard, and MIT to provide online learning experiences similar to those found on campuses. Will hybrid degrees— awarded for a mix of on-campus and online learning—emerge as a new, time-saving, more economical alternative? Will young people begin entering the workforce earlier, as they do in Europe, earning degrees through co-op placements or evening studies? In one divergent idea, Paypal's billionaire co-founder Peter Thiel pays a yearly crop of twenty-two promising, entrepreneurial high school graduates $100,000 each to delay college for two years, simply to see if it will help him find the next breakthrough idea. This much is certain: The current model is unsustainable, and when change strikes, it will be divergent and it will likely render obsolete vast numbers of universities and colleges. Opportunities include entrepreneurial education, gamified learning, lifestyle education, virtual classrooms, technology-enabled education, and resurgence of practical and vocational education.

ADVERTISING AND MARKETING Data-driven advertising is here to stay. Today, we still largely view ads as a nuisance, but as advertisers better understand our habits, mobile location, and purchasing patterns, we'll be more likely to be presented with the right product at the right time for the right price. Consider this potential scenario: A jeweler in San Francisco could design a Facebook ad campaign targeted toward single males aged twenty-three to twenty-eight who've been in a relationship for a few years but aren't yet engaged. These young men are far more likely to be the jeweler's ideal customer than the average person walking past billboards on the street. We aren't far away from the scenario in the movie *Minority Report* in which individualized ads pop out at just the right place and time. Marketers are also recognizing that in an ad-cluttered marketplace, the quickest way to stand out from the crowd is to be refreshingly divergent and unique. Opportunities include interactive advertising, personalized targeting, personalized ads, sampletising (which is our word for customers test-driving a product before buying it), brands as media, socially responsible branding, transparency campaigns, and a rise in branding.

CONCLUSION

I f you take away only one message from this book, I hope it will be that the only real certainty in life is change.

Only by awakening your inner hunter and looking for patterns will you be better equipped to adapt and thrive in the face of this change. As we've seen in so many different fields, the journey starts with recognizing—and avoiding—the three traps of the farmer and then pivoting to an all-out hunt for the six patterns of opportunity.

For me, writing this book has been a personal journey. My father's entrepreneurial accomplishments were a huge source of inspiration; he taught me to hunt the world for ideas, searching for overlooked opportunity, and I, in turn, created an online community that helps individuals do just that. Then, as I worked on the final chapters, I had to struggle with his death. Painful as it was, I more clearly see the connection between my ambitious path and the influence of my entrepreneurial father, relentlessly supportive mother, and cancer-conquering older sister.

After all this talk about patterns, it seems fitting to realize that all of us are the consequence of how we respond to the patterns in our environment.

So, in parting, I would urge you to think of that sea turtle mentioned at this book's beginning. There will be many times that you'll feel randomly off course, but pay attention to the ebbs and flows. Just keep the following three principles in mind, and you'll find your way back every time.

Be curious.

Be willing to destroy.

Be insatiable.

Appendix: Case Studies

HOW TO LAUNCH A RESTAURANT IN 30 DAYS

Have you ever dreamed of opening your own restaurant or bar? Whether you have or not, let's use this example as a mental exercise to see just how the patterns you've learned about in this book can be put into action. So do me a favor and fast-forward your life and imagine that you've quit your job. But you're too vital and creative to simply retire. So you decide to open a restaurant. How would you choose the cuisine? Would you serve fast food, or would you aim for fine dining? What about drinks and décor? Would you tie everything together with a theme? What would that theme be?

Before reading further, take a moment to gather your thoughts and commit to your restaurant idea . . .

In all likelihood, you've come up with an interesting restaurant concept, but experience tells me that you can do better. It goes back to what I mentioned before: Your first ideas will likely be rooted in gut instinct or some notions you picked up while eating at your favorite restaurants. People tend to base decisions on past experience. They farm. Because you've eaten at hundreds of restaurants and consider yourself to have developed homegrown expertise on this subject, your brain fools you into thinking that you have the experience and tools to produce a compelling restaurant concept.

In the story that follows, you'll see how a robust and thorough approach to hunting—rather than farming—can result in a restaurant that is more noteworthy and more likely to succeed.

Sang Kim is Toronto's king of sushi, though you wouldn't guess it by looking at his bohemian attire, felt fedora, knitted sweaters, and thick, retro glasses. The Korea-born Kim rose to culinary stardom after helping to launch such hot sushi destinations in downtown Toronto as Ki, Blowfish, and Koko Share Bar. But the thing is, he never actually opened his *own* restaurant. That dream had cooled on the back burner, especially with the success of his consulting career and sushi courses. Then, in March 2012, he received an intriguing call from a friend. There was a vacancy at a prime corner location on Baldwin Street, a restaurant-filled lane off of Toronto's busy Spadina Avenue, which is celebrated as one of the city's fine dining centers.

Kim wasn't looking to start a new restaurant. He didn't have the time. He knew it would take him the better part of a year to dream up a concept, theme a menu, and craft a marketing plan. Though he politely declined, he *was* tempted. The location was excellent, and he thought it could be fun, so the idea kept calling to him.

Whether you're an entrepreneur or just someone with good ideas and not enough hours in the day, you know that feeling. You have this dream of launching a company or developing a new product, but there always seem to be reasons not to do it; whether it's fear of failure or lack of time, money, or resources, something is holding you back.

After weeks of thinking of little else but the potential restaurant of his dreams, Kim finally agreed to at least *look* at the property. But when he did give it a walk-through, he discovered that the space had previously housed a tacky former chicken wing franchise. The deep fryers, neon beer signs, and cheap furniture were a world apart from the fine restaurants he'd already created, and he couldn't imagine how to transform it into the kind of enterprise befitting his name and reputation. Seemingly intractable issues heightened the challenge. Kim didn't have the time to open a new restaurant, let alone build a new one from scratch. The current layout suggested a bar more than an eating establishment, and there was a large, unusable second space. Kim saw that the space had the potential to house two different restaurants. But he wasn't even sure he wanted to create *one*.

HOW WOULD *YOU* DO IT?

Put yourself in Kim's shoes. Would you make the leap? For Kim, the safe choice would be to keep doing what he'd done best: letting others take the financial plunge while consulting them to near-certain success. But on the other hand, by embracing risk, he'd have the chance to achieve a lifelong dream to create a restaurant of his own. And he might just be the man to figure out how to launch a restaurant in a snap. But rather than keep farming the same land as chef and consultant, Kim decided to hunt for something bigger and better. Here's how.

Step 1: Awaken—Escalate Commitment and Apply Pressure

After deliberating for what seemed like ages, Kim pulled the trigger. He worried that he was gambling, but, like any good hunter, he was insatiably curious. Plus, he had a strategy for mitigating the risk. Instead of devoting a year of his life to building the restaurant, Kim would create urgency by challenging himself to attempt something extraordinary. He'd dream up and launch *two* restaurants in one location—and pull it all off in just thirty days.

Was that remotely possible? Kim worried that he might be inviting a spectacular failure. But if he *could* pull it off, it would be his biggest feat yet. Within the week, he was committed. He inked his five-year lease, putting at stake hundreds of thousands of dollars.

The pressure sank in. Kim began to second-guess himself.

Excitedly, his friend asked if he had a concept in mind. Kim viewed the question as narrow-minded. So many diverse elements were involved in creating a successful new restaurant. You didn't just order a concept off a menu, and he knew better than to farm his past experience. Top restaurants require innovative approaches to menu, design, and ambience, which are far more likely to come from methodically hunting for ideas than from a single flash of insight.

Still, Kim had reason to worry. Most new restaurants fail, especially in a competitive metropolitan city such as Toronto, where, on occasion, as many as a dozen new restaurants may close their doors in a single week.

To start the ball rolling, Kim posted a giant question mark on his new building, along with this URL: HowToCreateARestaurant In30Days.com.

The rebel was throwing his hat in the ring, flaunting the craziness of his challenge. Could he develop a fresh concept, construct a landmark restaurant, hire a staff, and launch in just a month? It seemed impossible. But there it was, for anyone to follow and comment on online in Kim's daily blog. This public declaration garnered ideas and engagement from the crowds, and it also helped keep Kim committed and accountable.

With the clock ticking, Kim did something crazy. He flew to his home city of Seoul, South Korea, to immerse himself in the latest foods and trends, hunting for that unpredictable spark.

He knew that most restaurants fail because their owners don't bother to develop a fresh concept. Yes, it was insane to fly halfway around the world when he had less than a month before opening. But Kim thought it was his only chance.

TAKEAWAYS

1. **Pull the Trigger** Kim took action by defining his plan and committing himself financially.

2. **Create Urgency** He set a tight timeline, which made his quest a bigger challenge.

3. **Create Public Accountability** By creating public accountability, he put his reputation at stake. This increased his commitment and helped to channel the weight of his full network of support.

Step 2: Hunt—Force Yourself to Scour the World for Inspiration

Kim's first stop in Korea was Gangnam, the trendy, upscale district made famous by Park Jae Sang's (known as PSY) massively popular video "Gangnam Style." Think New York's Fifth Avenue or London's High Street. The insatiable (in both senses of the word) Kim ate his way through Gangnam's hottest spots, sampling a dozen meals a day.

He was underwhelmed.

Tasting "what's hot now" wasn't sparking breakthroughs. Kim branched out to other districts, looking for new patterns. He ate weird animals and rare fish, and he even sampled sannakji, a live squid dish popular in South Korea. The freaky appeal is that the tentacles latch onto your esophagus, creating an asphyxia that brings some quirky diners delight.

Kim knew that asphyxiation by live squid wouldn't fly in Toronto, but he also knew breakthrough opportunities are best discovered when you open your mind to what could be. Just as I learned at Capital One to test all sorts of arcane financial products, Kim needed to taste the full range of food possibilities.

Time was running short, though, so Kim thought back to how he'd first fallen in love with cooking. A memory came to him of being surrounded by women in his grandmother's kitchen. Those ladies loved food and argued passionately about ingredients, flavors, and even the ideal number of dishes for a meal. Recalling those happy childhood days, Kim realized that his Gangnam adventures had been on the wrong track. In a flash, he saw that instead of trying to hunt for what was trendiest *now*, he could tap into the power of cyclicality and divergence; in other words, he could mine his past for flavor and theme, and he could spin those concepts into a new, modern restaurant. Old-school street food was incredibly popular in Seoul. With growing excitement, he realized that he could draw on that nostalgic appeal and the atmosphere it created for his new restaurant. He would feature everything from "authentic cooking" to a "chef's table" reminiscent of a street vendor's counter. He began mapping out a nostalgic Korean restaurant and café with healthy ingredients. Memories of his mom's home cooking also sparked an idea for his smaller space: Perhaps he could draw students from nearby Toronto art schools with affordable pricing.

His excitement building, he quizzed a clutch of Korean students about their favorite food (remember the power of curiosity). When they joyfully cheered a dish called "Duk Bok Ki" (imagine rice gnocchi with Korean toppings), he asked them to take him to their favorite destinations. He treated them to every possible variety of food, and he instantly had a marvelously engaged focus group. He was excited by Duk Bok Ki, but more specifically, he was excited about the idea of nostalgia and he wanted to take it further—instead of just a single dish, he could expand the concept to blend all kinds of nostalgic Korean and American foods. He smiled as he considered that he might be the first person to make a bulgogi (grilled, marinated beef) cheeseburger, wasabi-spiked mac and cheese, and squash rice cakes.

Reality sank in, though, as he boarded a plane back to Toronto.

How would he overcome the fierce Toronto restaurant competition and impress the often hostile food critics? He started thinking about how our younger days are filled with competition and games. Could he converge this with the popular trend of reality cooking shows? Sitting in his airplane seat, he conceived a contest to be called Yakitori Top Chef. Eight chefs would each be invited to invent four skewers for a unique eponymous yakitori platter, showcasing their signature flavors.

The game couldn't be simpler: The winning top-selling chef could keep his or her skewers on the menu for the next three months. Meanwhile, seven new chefs would rotate in to battle against the winner for top spot. Participating chefs would get a cut of the profits and free promotion.

But Kim's brainstorming wasn't over. In another brilliant convergence of present and past, he decided to transform the front of his restaurant into a sushi school. Along the bar, he'd place a long row of tables capable of fitting twenty students before his digital chalkboard, a seventy-two-inch screen loaded with videos that he'd use to personally showcase his favorite lessons. Included in the content: Kim's colorful stories of the history of sushi. He envisioned a retro, immersive experience for large groups seeking to go "backstage" into the kitchen.

Kim shows us how identifying cyclical patterns can be as easy as dialing into your own past. Though your past may be different from your customer's, the feelings invoked are similar: comfort, warmth, and longing. The pull of nostalgia and retro is that you can tap into decades of preference and fond memories, putting you on the fast track to consumer love.

TAKEAWAYS

1. **Look Outside of Your Market** In pursuit of ideas, Kim actively relocated himself into a different culture and new frame of mind.

2. **Don't Limit Yourself to a Single Way of Hunting** When Kim failed to find the inspiration he expected, he quickly modified his plan, seeking out additional patterns—particularly nostalgia—to cue new ideas.

3. **Look Beyond the Possible** Kim extended his hunt beyond the limits of what seemed possible, including foods that might never work in North America, because he wanted to explore the full spectrum of possibilities.

Step 3: Capture—Make It Happen

Kim had overcome many of the initial obstacles, but he still needed to push hard to make the last critical steps happen.

During the final week of Kim's thirty-day challenge, some of his invited competitor chefs came to test their Yakitori Top Chef entries. Not surprisingly, they were a bit shocked to find that there was still no kitchen. Not only that, walls still needed to be demolished, pipes were still protruding, and Kim's liquor license had yet to be approved. "I could barely climb out of bed this morning, buried under an avalanche of fatigue," he blogged. "I think it may have something to do with the gathering momentum of impressions, ideas, conversations, emails, interviews, complaints—all of it coming down on me with increasing force every day."

He desperately needed to light a fire under his team of construction workers and suppliers. Critics doubted that his restaurant would open on time. Amazingly, though, Kim's two-business restaurant, called Yakitori, and the Seoul Food Company, opened its doors on the thirtieth day. Not everything was in place, but thanks to the

Yakitori Top Chef entries, the food was great. In the weeks that followed, Kim's restaurant received all the buzz and attention a chef could hope for.

Since then, dozens of celebrity chefs have competed in Kim's Yakitori Top Chef challenge, the restaurant has been rated by *USA Today* as one of Toronto's top restaurants, and Kim's sushi school has taught more than a thousand classes.

Kim's remarkable success reminds us that riding the right synergistic trends at the right time matters. Kim wisely tapped into the cyclical pattern of opportunity, channeling nostalgia and our fascination for retro delights that invoke our past, including our love of playful competition.

TAKEAWAYS

1. **Use Your Critics' Doubts as Fuel** Kim's project brought him to the edge of exhaustion, but the skepticism of others made him more determined to succeed.

2. **Launch Now, Fix Later** Kim had surprisingly few ideas in place before he began. But his emphasis on speed prevented him from getting bogged down by details or the enormity of the task.

3. **Collaborate** Like many innovators, Kim was pushing beyond his experience. By audaciously enlisting his competitors to help him, he was able to meet his self-imposed challenge.

HOW TO EDUCATE THE WORLD

Taylor Conroy lives by the motto "destroy normal," which, not surprisingly, is also the title of his blog. True to his mantra, the blond adventure addict sports a giant tattoo of a phoenix on his arm. Just like J. K. Rowling, he believes in the power of creative destruction.

At twenty, Conroy was determined to become a firefighter, but once he achieved his dream, he discovered that sitting around and waiting for a fire to fight wasn't the rush he expected. At twenty-one, he took the unusual step of committing 10 percent of his income to charity. He was still $15,000 in school debt, but he felt that donating a portion of his earnings to a good cause would add meaning to his life. "It didn't take long until I loved giving that money away. I felt like I was contributing, like I was doing my part, bettering the world. Even though it was only about $200 a month."[1]

Soon the insatiable young firefighter wanted more. He studied for a real estate license, and by twenty-four, he was licensed and working for RE/MAX in the sunny retirement mecca of Victoria, British Columbia.

Like the phoenix, he'd reincarnated himself.

Conroy quickly became the firm's top-grossing rookie agent in North America. He always made sure to save money for charity, which he'd pass to his friend, whose church seemed like a worthy

---

1 Taylor Conroy, "One CRUCIAL Money-Making Activity That 99.9% of People Miss," *Destroy Normal.*

recipient. One Sunday, his friend invited him to attend a sermon, and afterward, the pastor handed Conroy an envelope with his tax receipt. Conroy was shocked to discover that he'd donated $25,000!

He couldn't believe his eyes. His savings plan had ballooned into something truly meaningful. In a short time, he became addicted to the thrill of making money—and then giving it to a worthy cause. Over the next three years, his real estate franchise grew into a multimillion-dollar venture. He bought a seaside house and a fast motorbike, dated beautiful women, and placed third in a bodybuilding challenge. He traveled to thirty-three countries, surfed the world's longest wave in Peru, trained as a yoga teacher, and ran with the bulls in Spain. By this point, he'd given away several hundred thousand dollars and had another large sum to donate. He flew to Kenya to look for worthy candidates. He expected to find a suitable charity, return home, and send the charity checks for the foreseeable future. He expected to be able to *buy* his happiness.

But the cheerful kids he was befriending didn't fit his preconceptions of African poverty. These children were happy, but they were also oblivious to the pain and suffering that lay ahead. Half were infected with AIDS and likely to die in a few years. Many lacked the education to pull themselves out of economic catastrophe. Suddenly, his quest for a suitable place to make donations to took on greater urgency. In the midst of searching for a place where his money could have maximum impact, he stumbled across Free the Children, an organization that builds schools for roughly $9,000 each. Over the course of twenty years, each school has the potential to educate 1,000 kids, teaching them reading, writing, and math while making them aware of important social issues, such as gender equality.

Conroy immediately cut a check to build his first school. But after that school was built and he'd settled back into his regular routine of selling real estate, his thoughts were still consumed by the children he'd met. Grocery stores reminded him of wasted

food, while schoolyards made him realize how we often take education for granted. More driven than ever, he was now fully ready to
change the world.

But how?

HOW WOULD *YOU* DO IT?

Conroy spent the next year and a half hunting for his idea. Though
he wasn't exactly sure how his charitable venture would unfold, he
was motivated by three goals:

1. **Destroy Normal** Conroy was willing to destroy his current career
   because he knew he was meant to serve an altruistic purpose.

2. **Learn Your Market** Conroy was no expert in charity, but he'd spend
   every spare moment studying charities and business models to
   try to better understand what works.

3. **Explore New Possibilities** Conroy didn't imagine his concept would
   be similar to ideas that already existed. He'd need to research
   more than just charitable donations to find his inspiration.

With his inner hunter ready to pounce on ideas, Conroy began
his quest. At times, he had doubts. He wondered whether he should
stay with his profitable business, but he continued to feel called to
create a sustainable social venture. He explained to me that he knew
he had to create an "economic engine for social good."

His first step was to survey the terrain. He learned that three
trends have been dominating modern fundraising:

1. **Experiential Giving** Galas, art shows, raves, marathons, and golf
   tournaments all expose people to a charity's underlying premise.
   But these models struck Conroy as wasteful because the char-

ity was in the background, and event costs could spiral out of control.

2. **Street Solicitation** The latest craze among fundraisers is to dispatch paid solicitors to downtown street corners, where they try to "hard sell" pedestrians on a cause. This approach *can* be highly effective, but it's expensive and it often annoys people.

3. **Shockvertising** Prospective donors are shown an image of a child near death with a tear in his or her eye, and people feel compelled to donate. Conroy hated how this type of "shock imagery" dehumanized victims.

Put yourself in Conroy's shoes for a moment, and think about the natural process a hunter might employ in this situation. By understanding popular new trends, Conroy could target the patterns of opportunity to create something different. He began by zeroing in on the most powerful and contagious aspect of a charity challenge, and he quickly got excited about the simple concept of giving along with your friends and making it an enjoyable communal experience. Conroy explained to me, "When I knew I was creating a school, I felt, 'this is awesome' and I wanted a way to get my friends to feel the same way."

To prototype his friendship-giving concept, he launched a $2,500 giving-with-friends experiment. Conroy sent each of his twenty-five closest friends a $100 check in the mail. Pick a favorite charity, he suggested, add additional funds if you want, and then share what you do with the donations on Facebook. Most of Conroy's friends matched the donation, and one even turned the $100 into $800.

This first successful experiment proved that friends *do* like giving together and that Conroy could turn $2,500 into $6,000—close to the cost of building a school.

Divergence Pattern

Because none of the three status quo trends in giving appealed to Conroy, he sought a divergent business model. This led him to "Challenge Fundraising." Groups would create their *own* social businesses, giving them ownership of the process and the satisfaction that comes with it.

As Conroy searched for a way to test such a challenge, Christina Pelletier, a local schoolteacher and friend, invited him to bring his competition to her classrooms. With $1,800 of seed money, Conroy challenged eighteen classes in one of Victoria's elementary schools to see what business they could create with $100 of start-up capital. He hoped each classroom could generate $500, enough to fund a $9,000 school. Classes launched everything from a simple muffin business to a mini soap factory. The kids in what Conroy called his "Early Entrepreneurs Experiment" doubled their goal, funding *two* new $9,000 schools—while giving 400 students an inspirational, real-life lesson in entrepreneurship and philanthropy.

Acceleration Pattern

In his third experiment, Conroy boiled down the most successful element of his project with the kids: the competition. Would it work online, he wondered? Conroy zeroed in on the competition aspect and sought to accelerate it. Since competition seemed to inspire excellence, he challenged his blog readers to tell him the best way to turn $1,000 into $5,000. And he offered to bequeath his frequent-flier points to whoever dreamed up the top idea, promising to send the winner anywhere in North or South America.

The winning idea was a twist on the popular model of soliciting pledges for running races or walking events. One woman asked forty-two friends to donate the price of a Starbucks latte, $4.20, for forty-two days ($176.40 each). This, combined with Conroy's $1,000 seed money, funded a $9,000 school.

Reduction Pattern

Conroy loved how this new strategy simplified and encouraged giving. Asking friends to donate the price of a coffee a day for just over a month seemed to connect with people. The concept inspired Conroy to dream up a new idea. Though he remained unsure of what method to pursue, his experiments had yielded three important insights:

1. **Friendship Giving** Conroy proved that this strategy worked, and he wanted to accelerate it.

2. **Challenge Philanthropy** By narrowing in on status and competition, Conroy could create a concept that diverged from the mainstream and would be successful—as the school kids had proven.

3. **Simplification** Making a simple and tangible request had been extraordinarily successful at getting friends to chip in.

Convergence Pattern

One day, while doodling ideas on his whiteboard, Conroy realized that he needed to intentionally reject traditional fundraising tactics. He countered with a scheme that converged all three of his main insights. He called it Change Heroes. His idea was to create a social platform that would enable people to send personalized videos to their friends. Imagine receiving this e-mail from a friend: "Thanks for having me over the other day. I have an idea that I think you are going to love. Check out this video I made for you: http://www.ChangeHeroes.com/Jeremy-and-XYZs-School" (where "XYZ" is your name, of course). People don't generally send personalized videos, so this message would break through the clutter of your busy inbox. You'd click on it and see a customized video—and the ability to donate.

But there was a technical hurdle. Conroy needed to create a platform to let people easily record thirty-three intro videos on their webcam to send to thirty-three friends. And he wanted the videos to automatically splice together with Change Heroes videos from Kenya. He also wanted to track when people watched their videos and to allow integrated communication so that people participating in the Change Heroes effort could follow up with their friends with the click of a button.

Conroy contacted Elton Pereira, a developer who was so enthused by the project that he jumped right into it. A few weeks later, Pereira called Conroy and said, "It's up and it works." Conroy told Pereira that he was thrilled to learn that he could now test it out. "No, I mean it already works," Pereira replied. "I *did* test it!" In two days, Pereira had raised enough money to fund two more schools.

Conroy's world was once again about to change. His hunt resulted in an extraordinary opportunity, and now he'd have to make a decision about how to fully exploit it.

He realized that his Change Heroes platform was remarkable. One day, he looked out his office window at the skyline of condos and houses he might one day sell. He told me, "I had this moment where I thought, *How am I going to feel a year from now if I sell five hundred more properties, but wonder if I could have made an even bigger difference?*"

Conroy called a meeting with his two real estate business partners and asked them what their goals for the future were. His first business partner wanted more time off. His second business partner wanted to lower costs and take home more money. Conroy said, "I want to do charity full time."

To his surprise, they were ecstatic and supportive, and he was able to craft a fair buyout.

Conroy was now a full-time Change Hero.

In its first year, Change Heroes raised one million dollars and funded one hundred schools. That changed the lives of 100,000 students. Conroy has subsequently spoken at the United Nations, the Harvard University Social Enterprise Conference, and New York University. Inspired by his new way of life, he told me, "People forget how easy it can be to learn new things and find new ideas, but you actually have to push yourself to look. Whether the goal is to change the world or find a new business idea, we're all capable of much more than we might think."

Acknowledgments

Sig Gutsche: It was a difficult year, but I feel fortunate to have interviewed you just weeks before you passed. I didn't realize it till after you were gone, but I see now that Trend Hunter is ultimately the digital evolution of our weekly endeavor to scour the world for business ideas.

Kyla Gutsche: For triumphing through adversity and creating such a remarkable business that has transformed the lives of so many people. Through your story in this book, I hope to encourage others with your inspirational approach to life.

Shelby Walsh: For all the ways you've made this book, our company, and my life better as Trend Hunter's head of research, president, and my better half. Thanks for "saying yes" during the course of this book.

Jonathan Littman: For your editorial work on the book and its structure. You've helped to polish the stories and—true to your brand—snowball the overall quality of the book.

Rick Horgan: For being a relentless executive editor and upping my game to the next level. Your vision not only reshaped the direction of the book, but also my approach to keynotes and use of personal stories to more deeply convey the message.

Tina Constable: For your excitement and support as the publisher from day one right to the completion of this exciting book!

Talia Krohn: For your enthusiasm, editorial polish, and clever work launching the book.

Jaime Neely: For your exceptional work as Trend Hunter's senior editor and the research lead on this project. You've discovered some of the book's best stories and are amazing at your career.

Armida Ascano: For shining your positive energy on the book (and our office) as one of Trend Hunter's leaders and one of the most colorful writers on this roller coaster we call life.

Courtney Scharf: For all your ideas integrating Trend Hunter's client work and insight into the prose while adding your own clever zest.

Katherine Vong: For diving into hundreds of business stories as part of the book's early research, and continuing the project even after you departed Trend Hunter for business school.

Gil Haddi: For being fearless at landing interviews with some of the most difficult to reach people on the planet.

Jonathon Brown: For your ambitious team work, stunt doubling, and architecture of the book launch.

Misel Saban: For your incredible flexibility and charisma while managing *Better and Faster*'s publicity.

Trend Hunter's Full-Time Team and Top Contributors: For nuggets of gold and terrific stories. Special thanks to Taylor Keefe,

Andrew Chow, Michael Hemsworth, Tana Makmanee, Derek Cohen, Sarah St. Jules, Thomas Wade-West, Meghan Young, Jana Pijak, Laura McQuarrie, Alyson Wyers, Anne Booth, Farida Helmy, Vasiliki Marapas, Jamie Munro, Rahul Kalvapalle, Jordy Eleni, Amelia Roblin, Michael Hines, Bianca Bartz, Jacob Courtade, Katie Pagnotta, and Marissa Brassfield.

Gillian MacKenzie: For being the best book agent in the business. You are always an amazing ally in this big world of publishing.

Ayelet Gruenspecht, Megan Perritt, Derek Reed, and Campbell Wharton: For amazing enthusiasm and guidance with the editing details and launch of *Better and Faster.*

For all those who helped Trend Hunter with their interviews and advice, including: Robert Lang (origami), Diane von Furstenberg (DVF), Hans Vriens (Red Bull), The Victoria's Secret Team, Ron Finley (Gangster Gardener), Jake Bronstein (Flint and Tinder), Steve Sasson (Kodak, inventor of the digital camera), Sharon DiFelice (Crayola), Ned Loach and Robert Gontier (360 Screenings), David Horvath (Uglydoll), Nicole DeBoom (Skirt Sports), Matt Schnarr (Awake Chocolate), Sophia Amoruso (Nasty Gal), Micha Kaufman (Fiverr), Josh Opperman (I Do Now I Don't), Robert Hintz and Greg Hodge (Beautiful People), Stephen Gold (IBM), Sang Kim (Yakitori), and Taylor Conroy (Change Heroes).

And, of course, our loyal Trend Hunter readers and clients who have shaped the insights of the book while helping us to battle-test business theories using the power of big data.

Index

Take Your Idea Hunt to the *Next* Level

To redeem, go to BetterAndFaster.com

BETTER AND FASTER will teach you to find your next idea, and then we want to actually help you find it! This unique code entitles you to bonus material:*

1. Understand Your Traps with a Self-Assessment
2. Get Special Access to the #1 Database of Ideas
3. Watch Inspiring *Better and Faster* Keynote Videos
4. Get Sample Custom Research from Our Advisors

TRENDHUNTER™
FIND BETTER IDEAS, FASTER

Better and Faster
Frameworks

THREE STEPS TO DISRUPTION

I. **AWAKEN:** The Hunter vs. the Farmer

II. **HUNT:** The Six Patterns of Opportunity

III. **CAPTURE:** Find Your Idea

I. AWAKEN: The Hunter vs. the Farmer

Three Traps of the Farmer		Three Hunter Instincts	
🏆	Complacent ➤	✊	Insatiable
⚙	Repetitive ➤	🦁	Curious
🏰	Protective ➤	🦅	Willing to Destroy

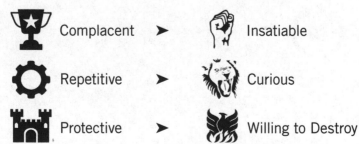

II. HUNT: The Six Patterns of Opportunity

Convergence
Align Multiple Forces
Physical + Digital
Converge People
Combine Brands
Add Value

Acceleration
Perfection
Aspirational Icon
Exaggerated Feature
Reimagined Solution

Redirection
Rationalizing/Refocusing
Reprioritizing
Reversing
Surprising
Gamifying

Cyclicality
Retro
Nostalgia
Generational
Economic
Seasonal

Reduction
Simplification
Specialization
Fewer Layers/Steps
Fractional
Crowding
Subscription
More Efficient

Divergence
Personalization
Customization
Status
Style
Exclusive Belonging
Generational Rebellion
Fashionizing

III. CAPTURE: Find Your Idea

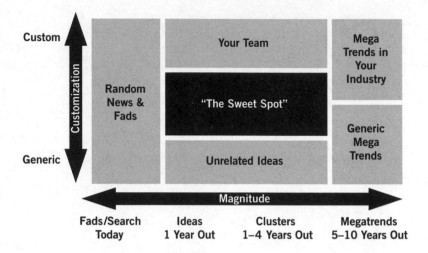

1. Awaken Your Hunter

2. Establish a Hunting Ground

3. Search the Perimeter for Slightly Related Ideas

4. Push Your Boundaries

5. Collect and Cluster What You Find

6. Throw Away Your First Clusters

7. Use the Patterns to Re-cluster

DOWNLOAD OUR FULL TOOLKIT
Get All the Printable References and
Frameworks at BetterAndFaster.com